Creatures of the Forest

Creatures of the Forest
Copyright 2018
Deborah Lee Davis

Note:
All these verses are in the King James Translation. Please look them up in several translations. When you find the one that speaks to you, print it out, post it around your house, read it out loud and make that Truth your own. If you don't see what you need here, please take the time to ask your pastor, friends, or even search the Internet. Search God's word. The Truth help you in every situation.

Published by Davis Mission
PO Box 215
Olean, NY 14760

Preface

Sometimes in life we find that our lives have taken detours through dark and troubling times. We struggle to see the light and sometimes even doubt that it exists. It is in this forest of darkness that we find thoughts of depression, inferiority, shame, unforgiveness, or jealousy, to name a few. These are the Creatures of the Forest.

Jesus came to bring his light into the darkness! All the Creatures of the Forest run and hide in his light. He is glowing with an intensity that causes all the evil spirits of hell to run for cover. In John 14:5-6, one of the twelve disciples named Thomas, asked Jesus, "How can we find the way?" You may be asking these same questions. "How do I find my way through dark times? How can I navigate through life when I'm going through so many troubles?"

The answer is simple. Truth! Believe the Truth. Receive the Truth. Meditate on the Truth. Jesus is Truth. He is the only way out of your troubles. He speaks Truth. He embodies Truth. He is Truth. Read the Word of God. Make it your own. Consume it and let it fill every last part of you. Replace all fear and condemnation with Truth. He is the light that shines in the darkness and nothing argues with Him.

Ask the Lord, to fill you with the Spirit of Truth. Allow Him to change your thinking. When you do, watch and see what miracles he does in your life!

TABLE OF CONTENTS

John 14:5-6

Thomas saith unto him, Lord, we know not whither thou goest; and how can we know the way? Jesus saith unto him, I am the way, the truth, and the life: no man cometh unto the Father, but by me.

John 14:15-17

If ye love me, keep my commandments. And I will pray the Father, and he shall give you another Comforter, that he may abide with you for ever; *Even* the Spirit of truth; whom the world cannot receive, because it seeth him not, neither knoweth him: but ye know him; for he dwelleth with you, and shall be in you.

Jesus is Truth
He is Creature Killing Truth

Chapter 1

Harriet Snelling

Harriet Snelling had been walking for hours. She had scurried from the backseat of the car as its driver had stopped to get gas. After having been held captive for the last forty-eight hours, she had lost all hope of escaping. It seemed like a miracle that the man was distracted and had left the doors unlocked. He probably didn't think she would even be able to escape after the torture she had been through. It certainly didn't seem like he even noticed that she was gone as he sped out of the gas station parking lot. Surely he would eventually notice she had escaped and would come back looking for her. All through the night she stumbled along, fear driving her to keep going, stopping only a few times to catch her breath.

Now the sun was just starting to come up and she realized that she was lost. Hours ago she chided herself for not asking for help back at the gas station. She was just so intent on getting away that she took off running. Not knowing what to do, coupled with the fact that she hadn't eaten in a long while, she started shaking. Great drops of tears started to fall from her face and she fell to the ground while her whole body trembled. "Oh God," what should I do? "Where should I go?"

Just then she heard some cows mooing in the distance and a spark of hope filled her heart. Maybe there was a farm nearby. Maybe, if she could follow the sound of the mooing, she would find someone who could help her. So she picked herself up from the heap she had fallen into, turned towards the sound, and started walking again. After about fifteen minutes she spied a little house nestled in the center of a dairy farm.

Ten minutes more found her sitting at the kitchen table drinking coffee. When she had knocked at the door she was greeted by the farmer's wife, who took one look at Harriet's bloody face and drew her inside. She was now on the telephone with the local police while Harriet nibbled on toast and sipped hot coffee.

It wasn't long before the police and an ambulance came. While the detectives took down all of Harriet's information, the paramedics were checking her vitals and strapping her to a back board for the ride to the hospital. She had several deep gashes on her legs that she couldn't even remember getting, a large cut and bruise on her forehead. These were all taken care of by the skillful care of the doctors and nurses in the emergency room.

What no one knew was, while the outside of her petite little body was healing quickly from her physical trauma, her mind was locked into a dark forest that wouldn't let her out. Living in that forest were little creatures. Everyday they tormented her. Like little wisps of thought they flew around her mind. Fast and with what seemed like an endless amount of energy, they blocked out all light. They loved the darkness of her thoughts and added to those thoughts whenever Harriet would listen to them.

ଔଔଔଔଔଔଔଔଔଔଔଔଔଔ

It had now been one year from the date that she had been abducted. She had been afraid of this day. As far as anyone knew, she was doing fine. Her abductor had been caught and sentenced to a long jail term. She had gone back to work at the bookstore and had even taken some painting classes at the local craft store. Life was back on track or so it seemed. A friend had taken her out to eat at her favorite restaurant for dinner and Harriet tried to eat and act like everything was normal but it wasn't. As soon as they finished eating Harriet asked her friend to drive her home. She had a splitting headache.

Walking into her dark and empty little house felt a bit creepy even though she knew no one was there. Suddenly her thoughts started to spin out of control and the forest consumed her. She stood rigid, unable to move because of the fear that had taken control. Over and over in her mind her thoughts raced. The creatures of the forest were putting on a show and she was their only audience.

Fear was the ringleader of this carnival. He had all of his friends on standby should he need them but he felt sure that he and his little Fearlings had Harriet well under their control. Around and round they flew encircling Harriet's mind with an invisible web much like a spider might do to his prey. He had plans to become lord of this forest, with the expectation that this would be his own little kingdom. He had no desire to let her go, as a matter of fact he was the architect of a whole new housing development. He was creating permanent homes for his family and friends in the forest of her mind.

The next day found her huddled on the floor in her living room. Her clothes crumpled and wet from her nightmares, clung to her body. She felt achy all over and the headache she had complained about the night before, was still raging. Her green eyes hurt when she tried to open them, so she squeezed them shut as she stood up. Staggering to her bed she clutched her phone. She had to call into work sick. There was no way she could make it in today. Fear was chuckling in the background. Yep, he had picked the right place to build his home.

The next anniversary was a bit less traumatic. Harriet had lost her dream job, which was a shame because she loved books. Fear had build his home just like he had wanted. There were several new generations of Fearlings who were living in Harriet's mind as well. The forest was a busy bee hive of Fearling life. These creatures reproduce at a very rapid rate when given attention and Harriet had given them a lot of attention.

She had tried to stop the dark thoughts but they wouldn't go away. She had seen many counselors and tried various drugs but none of them helped. She seemed powerless to fight the creatures in her mind. Night and day they would spin their webs. Some days she would feel like she had them under control and then, just when she thought her life would get back to normal, the Fearlings would rise up again and command her mind. Migraines plagued her and she stayed home from work so many times that her boss finally had to fire her. That was a sad day but a relief as well since now she wouldn't have to fight the dark thoughts and get ready for work. She could just stay in bed all day and no one would notice. It was a blessing that she had inherited her home and had a small inheritance from her parents when they died. She could just stay home, every day with the Creatures of the Forest.

Replace Your Thoughts By: Praying and Speaking Truth

Chapter 2
Stephen Foster

Stephen Foster had graduated from Brooks Glen high school with plans of going to the university on a football scholarship. A dislocated knee ruined that dream. His grades hadn't been that great, not because he wasn't smart but because he didn't think he needed to work hard at his studies. Solidly built and six foot two inches tall, he was the star player on the school's team. He was sure he had his scholarship in the bag. It was a bitter disappointment to lose it for sure, but Steve had learned that sometimes in life our plans change. His parents were firm believers that when a door closes, God has another plan. As much as it hurt to have his dream die, Steve refused to believe his life was over. He had seen too many athletes' careers destroyed by injuries. Since he couldn't get into his school of choice and not knowing what he should do with his life he decided to spend a year at a little Bible school in the mountains of North Carolina. Ten years later he was still there. He had graduated from the school and stayed on as the Dean of Students. No, it wasn't what he thought his life would become but he loved it.

Then suddenly his life took another abrupt change. His father, who had been the picture of health, had a brain aneurysm and had passed away in the night. His mother needed him. So packing up his belongings and saying goodby to his students, he drove the ten hour long trip home.

The little house that had been his home for so many years, was full of people comforting his mom. When they noticed Steve walk in, they surrounded him as well, hugging and offering condolences. He hadn't been home that much in the last few years but he was still one of them and they were happy to see him. His mom Caroline, was sitting in the rocker by the window that had always been her favorite place to sit. She had a crooked smile that spoke volumes to Steve. Her heart had been broken by her loss and her blue eyes threatened to spill over. She was so relieved to have Steve home. She stood to wrap her arms around her tall son and breathe in the smell of his golden brown hair that was so much like his dad's.

"I wish you could have seen him one last time Steve, he was so proud of you." She said as she gave him one last fierce hug and sat back down in her chair.

Steve sat on the stool next to her and taking her hand said, "Yea mama, I know. I wish I could have seen him too but we both know where he is and we will see him again someday." They both nodded their heads at that and together they stared off in the distance to another time and place where they would see their loved one again.

After a few minutes of silence Steve's mom said, "You know, they want you to take your dad's place in the church. They loved your dad so much and the whole church is grieving. You will stay won't you?"

Nodding his head yes, he said, "Yea mom, Jack Massey called me right after you did. He told me the church wanted me to take dad's place. We have a meeting with the church board all set up for tonight. Don't worry momma. I'll take care of everything. I already packed my things. Everything is in the car. Is my old room still available?"

Of course it was.

Six months later the mother and son had settled into a routine. The church had continued to run smoothly with few changes. Steve had added some special nights of prayer and the folks who attended had grown into a powerful prayer team. He had felt the Holy Spirit prompt him to especially pray for direction. He knew in his heart that coming home was the right thing to do but he wanted to have a specific plan. Because of his unsettled feelings, he had started the special prayer meetings. Hopefully the Lord would bring direction from them. It was only after a few weeks that he noticed a pattern in everyone's prayers. They were praying for TRUTH.

Stella Farrell was the first to pray for truth. With golden hair and a youthful face she seemed much younger than she was. The sixty-nine year old was down on her knees crying when she started to shout, "Lord your word says that Jesus is the way the truth and the life. People in this city need to find the way to you. They want so many things in this life but what they really need is your truth! The truth will set them free and lead them to you Lord Jesus. Then they will have life. Lord, you are the truth. Show us the truth. Show us how to bring the truth to our little city. Lord how can we reach anyone if we can't see or even hear the truth for ourselves?"

One by one that same prayer continued until everyone was consumed by it. Weeks went by and the same prayer was on everyone's lips. Sarah Handler, another of the older ladies in the group, printed some little cards that said, "The TRUTH will set you free." Some she laminated and then put a magnet on the back. Everyone had one stuck to their refrigerator. Kevin Knowls, the owner of the local hardware store, had taken a handful of them and was passing them out at his cash register, to everyone who came in. Susie Crandall had printed her own and was taping one to her pastry boxes when people bought donuts at her coffee shop. Mike Tenor stapled his to every invoice at his landscaping business.

Several of the pastors in town had heard about the prayer meetings and wanted to join in. What had started out as a little prayer meeting became a city wide prayer movement that was attacking what would soon be known as, the Creatures of the Forest.

Jesus is Truth
He is Creature Killing Truth

Chapter 3

Roger and Lucy Woodard

Roger Woodard owned one of the city's auto mechanics shops. Working on cars was his passion. He loved the smell of new cars and the musty odor of the old ones. Looking under the hood of an antique car usually made his day but lately nothing made him happy. Lucy, his wife, had just asked for a divorce. It had never occurred to him that she was unhappy. In shocked silence he went about his day mumbling as he went. What happened? He had been a good provider. They weren't rich but they had a good life, or so he thought. What was it she had said? "I don't think you love me, and furthermore I don't love you any more?" Could that be true? She thought he didn't love her any more? How could she think that? He brought home a paycheck every week. Of course he loved her. He didn't drink a lot and he had never been unfaithful, well there was that one time when he had gone out with some guys on a hunting trip. Things did get a little carried away. His buddy Ben had brought several cases of beer with him. He had also invited some friends to come along. He hadn't bothered to tell the guys that his friends were women until they arrived. By then it was too late.

Other than that one weekend, Roger had been faithful. But memories of that time plagued his mind with guilt. The Forest was closing in on him and the creatures of that darkness spoke to him every day. Every time he kissed his wife or gave her a hug, feelings of guilt would torment him. It got so he couldn't bear to touch her because the pain of his betrayal was so great. The wispy creatures were so insidious. They knew how to hide and then come out of their dark caves at just the wrong time. Four months ago was Roger and Lucy's twentieth wedding anniversary. Lucy had been talking about it for months. First she wanted a party and a new dress. Then she wanted to go away on a trip, just the two of them. Roger reacted to the trip a little too strongly, with the help of the Guilties, "No! I'm not going away. We have a perfectly good bed at home. We don't need to go any place." It wasn't the trip that had him so upset. No, it was spending time alone on a romantic trip with his wife along with the Creatures of the Forest that had him upset. That night, Lucy left for her sister's and didn't come home for a week.

Roger gave in to the party but not to the trip. Guilty had tormented Roger to the point that he didn't sleep well. There was a whole choir of Guilties who sang to him as he would start to nod off. "Roger is guilty, guilty, guilty. And we will never go away. We are embedded in his memory and he can't forget. Guilty! Guilty! Guilty!" They even had a drummer to help beat the dark memories deeper and deeper. By the time the party came, Roger was a nervous wreck. When one of the guys from the hunting trip showed up at the party, he couldn't take his guilt any more and left. He grabbed a handful of clothes and some toiletries from the house and fixed a room in his shop to sleep. He tried to go home a few times but he just couldn't look at Lucy. The webs of Guilty had spun so tightly around his mind that even seeing her made him feel sick to his stomach. Oh if he could just forget that night but Guilty had carved a home deep in his mind.

Lucy couldn't remember when the last time was that Roger kissed her. Last year maybe? She knew she had gained some weight through the years. Was that why he didn't love her any more? Of course she still loved him but she wouldn't let him have the satisfaction of knowing that. Not when he so obviously didn't love her. She had her own Creatures of the Forest to deal with.

She had always felt a bit inadequate. She didn't think she was pretty but Roger used to tell her she was pretty. Now he wouldn't even touch her. Was she that repulsive? Was it the grey in her hair? The wrinkles on her face? She colored her hair and even bought some of the new wrinkle creams advertised on television. Losing weight wasn't so easy. She would lose a few pounds and then she would see that look on Roger's face. The look that told Lucy everything she needed to know, he didn't love her any more. So she would drown her sorrow in a pint of ice cream and forget about the diet till she was desperate enough to try again. Yo-yo dieting didn't fix anything it only made her unhappy.

Inadequate, Unloved, and Rejected were triplets in the forest of Lucy's mind. They were like a trio of trumpets blaring their horns from her mind to her heart, teasing her and ridiculing her until she thought she might break. Not only had they spun their web around her heart and mind but they had blinded her eyes as well. She couldn't see the pain on Roger's face when she asked for the divorce. The grimace that he wore, she interpreted as satisfaction. It was obvious to her that he was happy to finally be rid of her. When she started to cry he just turned away and never said a word. Was he that uncaring?

Roger slammed the hood of the car he was working on. He took his meaty fist and struck the car with such force that he put a dent in it. Guilty was busy calling his friend Anger. Obviously there would be room for him to camp out at Guilty's place tonight. Guilty would enjoy having a friend around.

That night Roger stopped by the corner store and picked up a six pack of beer. He was so mad. Anger had wings like a hummingbird and they hummed their tune with every flap, "How dare she ask for a divorce? How dare she? After twenty years. How could she think I didn't love her. Of course I love her. Well she doesn't love me any more. There must be another man in her life. She has been trying to fix herself up with a new hair color and some new clothes. Yep there must be someone else. How dare she?" Around and around the Creatures of the Forest spun their web.

Sometime after midnight when he wasn't thinking straight, Roger called his friend Ben, "Hey Ben, you remember the girls you brought on our hunting trip? Do you remember the one that I liked? Yea, Mandy. You couldn't give me her phone number could you?"

The Creatures of the Forest had a party that night. They would have a home with Roger for sure.

Replace Your Thoughts By: Praying and Speaking Truth

Chapter 4

Rejection

Lucy managed to get some sleep sometime after midnight. As soon as the sun started to peek through her windows she woke with a start and tried to rub the sleep from her hazel colored eyes. At first she thought she had just had a nightmare but she slumped in a heap on her bed when she realized it was no dream. She was getting a divorce. Roger didn't love her any more. Fidgeting with her wedding ring she let out a sigh. He never talked to her anymore. No matter how many times she asked him what he was thinking, he would always say, "Nothing." She had even begged him to tell her what was wrong but all he would say was, "Nothing." She thought for sure Roger would say he loved her. Surely when she threatened divorce it would force him to talk.

For the longest time she sat trying to understand what had just happened. She still loved him that was for sure but he obviously didn't love her. Rejection was lingering in her mind and the Darkness was closing in on her. "I'm fat. That's it, that's why he stopped loving me. He watched me try to lose weight and fail. He just doesn't love me. I'm not good enough for him anymore. Oh dear! What will the kids say?"

Spinning his web tightly around her mind, Rejection whispered in her thoughts. "He never did love you. You aren't lovable. You are worthless, worthless, worthless."

Trying to stop the downward spiral into despair, she turned on the television. Diet commercials with weight loss gimmicks flooded her living room. Sucked into their programming, she called the number on the screen and ordered a six month trial of herbal drink mixes that promised instant success. Then she turned the channel. A phone in psychic was offering to reveal secrets and in the process "change" your life. Lucy called that number too and paid a lot of money for nonsense. The woman on the other end of the phone said, "I feel you are sad. Are you sad? Yes? You have been hurt haven't you? Yes? It was your boyfriend, no your husband. Right?" After several of the woman's fishing excursions, Lucy hung up the phone. Was anything real any more? Her marriage wasn't real. That was for sure.

"Worthless. Worthless. Worthless," round and round the web of deceit was wound. The Creatures of the Forest were enjoying every minute.

It had been a couple of weeks since Lucy had been to church. She had stayed home the week before thinking Roger might go out for a Sunday brunch. The restaurant down the street was advertising a wonderful Sunday menu. She and Roger used to go out for Sunday brunch when they were first married. It was her last ditch effort to draw Roger out but when she called him at his shop, he wouldn't even get out of his makeshift bed to answer the phone. With a sigh Lucy gave up, made herself a cup of coffee and watched a church service on television.

The preacher on TV was one she normally liked but this particular Sunday morning the Creatures of the Forest were working double time. Hopeless and his friends were tormenting her tender heart so much that no matter how hard Lucy tried to follow what the TV preacher was saying, she just couldn't. Her mind spun out of control and after about fifteen minutes she clicked the remote to off and let the silent tears flow. That was the moment she decided to tell Roger that she wanted a divorce.

It was one week later and she didn't feel like going to church. She really didn't want to face people. Shame was whispering in her thoughts, "What will people think? I wonder if anyone knows about Roger and me? What should I say when people ask me how I'm doing? They will wonder where I was last week. I shouldn't go."

Then she realized she had to help in junior church. If only she had remembered last night, to call someone to take her place but no, she had forgotten.   She couldn't just stay home. Dear old Mrs. Shaker was visiting her son for the weekend and Lucy had promised to take her place. So, trying to rub away the cobwebs she felt in her brain, she put her hands to her face and let out a few weary breaths, stood, and went to get dressed.

An hour later with a travel cup of coffee in one hand and her keys in the other, she walked to her car and started her engine.   In that moment she realized she had forgotten something she had done every morning since she was a teenager. She hadn't prayed or even read one verse from her Bible all week. "Oh Lord, help me," she cried as she pulled out of her driveway.

Jesus is Truth
He is Creature Killing Truth

Chapter 5

Challenged By The Word

Washing up the dishes from their Sunday meal, Caroline turned and looked at her son, "It was a fine message you had for us today. I really felt challenged by the word. I have been wondering what I could do to be a better witness in our community. I don't feel like I have many talents. I was wondering, do you think one of my gifts from God is the ability to listen? I feel like I should invite some of the ladies who live down the street to come for tea. I could invite them one by one and just let them talk. Maybe they just need someone to listen. And then perhaps the Lord would give me the words and I could pray for them and show them who Jesus is. What do you think?"

Steve smiled and said, "Yes Mom you really do have the gift of listening. I think that is a great idea."

After the dishes were done, Caroline took out her pocket calendar, she still didn't understand the calendar on her new iPad, and penciled in some names on certain dates. Tomorrow morning she would start calling on her neighbors and see what kind of responses she would get.

Four weeks later, Caroline had made three new friends. Not everyone accepted the invitation from the Pastor's widow but the three who did, were quickly becoming her friends. Two were even going to church with her this morning. This was the second Sunday for Candice Lincoln. She loved it last week. She was forty years younger than Caroline. Her mom had died about five years ago and Caroline filled a need she had in her life. She had also grown up in the church but had not gone at all as an adult. Going with Mrs. Foster felt right to Candice. And she really liked listening to Pastor Steve.

This week Patsy Watson was joining them. She was the same age as Candice and had two toddlers in tow. Jumping in the back seat of Caroline's car, Patsy, two year old John, and three year old Susan settled in. "This is better than I imagined," Caroline thought as she pulled out of Patsy's driveway. Candice was chatting with the toddlers and it was easy to see these two young women might just become good friends.

The two kids in the back seat were giggling and Caroline smiled as she asked Patsy what they were saying. "They want to know if they can call you Mama Foster?" With a giggle of her own she nodded her head yes.

After Mama Foster dropped everyone off at the front door of the church, she drove around back to park. "Thank you Lord for my new friends. Thank you for those sweet little children. Lord use me somehow to make a difference in their lives."

ദ്രദ്രദ്രദ്രദ്രദ്രദ്രദ്രദ്രദ്രദ്രദ്രദ്ര

The local buffet in town was a popular place for church people to go for Sunday lunch. It was quite a multi denominational place as it seemed every church was represented. People would stop and linger to talk at other tables as they came and went from the buffet. No one talked doctrine here. There were two things everyone agreed on. One was food. The other were the prayer meetings. Truth meetings they were being called. They were still prayer meetings that is for sure but the emphasis of those prayers was truth. "Lord show us your truth!" was on everyone's lips. As a result, the Creatures of the Forest were scared. They lurked around every table, fearful of what they might hear yet unable to close their ears to the conversations happening around them in the restaurant.

Stella and Caroline had decided to take Candice and Patsy, along with her two toddlers to lunch. They were just getting the little ones strapped in their booster seats when Julie their waitress, stopped by to give them a hand. "Oh, hi Mrs. Foster," she said. "I didn't know you had grandchildren."

"I don't but if these two babies want to call me grandma, I don't mind."

Candice giggled. This was going to be a day to remember. She was having a great time. For the first time in a long while, she felt like she belonged. The whole table seemed wrapped up in the antics of the toddlers. Stella was spoon feeding apple sauce to John and Susan was picking the onions out of her plate of spaghetti. When no one was looking, she was dropping them off the side of her plate and on to the floor. What she didn't know was the onions were dropping right into Candice's designer hand bag. Patsy turned and saw the onions falling and started to discipline her little girl when Susan said, "But Mama, Auntie Candice won't mind. Do you Auntie Candice? Candice laughed so hard she thought she might pass out. But she caught her breath and said, "That's right Susan, Auntie Candice doesn't mind." She drew out the name, Auntie Candice, and started giggling again.

Several other patrons in the restaurant saw Susan and stifled their laughter. It was obvious that the restaurant was full of happy people. There was a new freedom among God's people and it seemed like everyone felt it. The Truth was working.

෬෬෬෬෬෬෬෬෬෬෬෬෬෬෬෬

One by one the dark and evil lurking thoughts gathered for a meeting of their own. How could they stop the prayer meetings? Something had to be done. They had been having so much success in the city that they thought they would live there for a very long time. However these prayer meetings were threatening their very existence. Every dark thought had ideas but the idea that seemed to please everyone the most, came from Deception.

Deception's father was Lies. He had grown up learning all the tricks of turning words and making people believe something that was not true. He knew how to ruin the prayer meetings. Divide the pastors that is the first thing to do. The second is to attack the families of the principal prayers. "We will whisper lies in their ears. By the time we are done with them, they won't know what hit them," he hissed!

Plans were made in detail. No one was left out. They all had jobs to do and fluttered out with little black puffs, spinning webs as they flew. The Creatures of the Forest were about to do battle and a bloody one it would be.

Replace Your Thoughts By: Praying and Speaking Truth

Chapter 6

Deception's Plan

Lucy Woodard parked her car right in front of the church and walked up the familiar steps. She was meeting with Pastor Steve. He had called her a few days ago wanting to set up an appointment. He had noticed her crying all through his message and then after church he heard the rumors that she and Roger were getting a divorce. She didn't really feel like opening her heart up to Pastor Steve. He was so young, just thirty years old and never married. How could he help? But she agreed to come.

Opening the front door, she walked in, never seeing Roger in his battered old pickup truck parked down the street. He thought there was another man in Lucy's life. Now he was sure of it. The other man was that new preacher at her church. He never did see what she saw in him. Week after week she would come home from church rehashing his messages as if they had come straight from God. Now he knew why. She was having an affair with that new preacher!

Deception was spinning a tale and Roger believed it all. It didn't take long and Deception had Roger all tied up in knots. Driving home, he began stewing about the whole situation. Here he had been feeling guilty about his unfaithfulness and now, come to find out, Lucy has been cheating on him the whole time. "Well, I'll teach her," he mumbled under his breath.

By the time he stopped at his buddy Ben's house, he had a plan. After a few beers and a lot of talk they went out to the local Walmart. Then later that night, armed with several cans of spray paint, they drove to Steve's church, and parked out back.

When the sun came up the next morning, the art work displayed on the church building was clear for all the world to see.

> Pastor Steve
> is not who you think he is
> He is having an affair
> with Lucy Woodard.
> Husbands watch your wives!
> Who's next?

It didn't take long before the whole town was abuzz about Pastor Steve and Lucy. Cars were backed up, slowly driving past the church just to see what all the commotion was about. Initially people rejected the idea but soon doubts arose and people didn't know what to think or who to believe. Gossips began to talk and once they did the Creatures of the Forest went to work.

Down at the local coffee shop, Steve was the topic of every conversation.

"You know, we don't know much about Pastor Steve. Don't you think it is strange that he never married?"

"I heard, just the other day, that Lucy and Roger are getting a divorce. This is probably the reason. I bet Roger caught her and that new pastor together. Why else would they get a divorce?"

"I saw Lucy walking into the church just yesterday. Can you believe it? And right under our noses."
Soon an emergency church board meeting was called for that very night. Unfortunately most people attending had already made up their minds as to whether Steve was guilty or not.

೮೮೮೮೮೮೮೮೮೮೮೮೮೮

Mother and son walked into the church together. Steve had an angry look to his face while his mother looked a little more worried. Nothing like this had ever happened before in their church. She really didn't know what to expect.

Eventually, most of the church board members believed Steve, especially when Lucy showed up. She was humiliated but convincing. No one really thought their young pastor would be attracted to the woman twice his age but stranger things had been known to happen. And the rumor mill loved a juicy story. Soon the talk was less about Steve and Lucy and more on to who had done the vandalism. There were speculations. Some people thought a local gang had done it. Others weren't so sure. What would the gang members gain by humiliating Lucy? But if not them, who? What motive did anyone have? Why single out Pastor Steve?

After everyone had gone home, they were no closer to finding the answers. As a matter of fact they had more questions. Unfortunately the rumor mill in town had just begun to churn. Fast food restaurants and coffee shops were filled with whispering patrons. Speculation and gossip were served up with every order of fries or cup of coffee. By the end of the day, the Creatures of the Forest had planted seeds in the minds of many in the city. Whereas pastor Steve had initially been accepted because of the love people had for his father, now many were unsure. Was he really a man who could be trusted? It was no surprise when few showed up for the next Truth prayer meeting. Many of the local pastors had called their members and told them that until they knew the truth, they would prefer if people stayed away from Steve's meetings. No one really knew what to believe.

Steve could almost feel the venomous whispers when he walked into the local cafe. He ordered a double espresso and a toasted bagel. He was going to eat there but changed his mind when he noticed people were staring at him. Normally he wouldn't have cared what people thought but this was so unfair, so untrue. He ordered his snack to go. When his order came, he went out of the side door, hoping he wouldn't have to talk to anyone.

Just as he was closing the door, he ran right into Pastor Mark. Mark was new to town. Where as Steve had grown up in the Glen, even though he had been gone for a long time, most people didn't see him as an outsider. Mark on the other hand was entirely new and many people still considered him an outsider. The two of them had become pretty good friends. Mark took one look at Steve and said, "Hey buddy, you look like you could use a friend."

"Boy could I," replied Steve.

A couple of hours and another double espresso later left Steve feeling much better. He always felt blessed to have Mark for a friend but never so much as at this time. Mark had practically forced Steve to sit at one of the outside tables belonging to the coffee shop. Steve had been so uncomfortable, feeling like the whole world was whispering about him, that he just wanted to get out of there. But Mark had insisted. He told Steve that he shouldn't give in to those feelings. After all, the rumors weren't true.

Then Mark opened his Bible to Song of Solomon 2:15. It said, "Take us the foxes, the little foxes, that spoil the vines: for our vines *have* tender grapes." He told Steve that the foxes were the thoughts Steve was fighting. "Set your mind on the Lord, Steve. Don't allow those little foxes to destroy everything the Lord has been doing these last few months. There is a spiritual battle going on and you are under attack. You know, thoughts have a way of coming to life and before you know it, they have stolen control. Like little creatures from deep in the forest they hide in the darkness and only come out when they feel that they are safe. Over and over they whisper words of anger, fear, hopelessness, you name it. Soon, the lies they tell seem like the truth and then we believe their lies."

Mark continued, "Steve, don't forget what the Apostle Paul said in 2 Corinthians 10." Opening his Bible he started to read. "For though we walk in the flesh, we do not war after the flesh: (For the weapons of our warfare *are* not carnal, but mighty through God to the pulling down of strongholds;) Casting down imaginations, and every high thing that exalteth itself against the knowledge of God, and bringing into captivity every thought to the obedience of Christ..."

All of a sudden, Steve's eyes lit up and it was like he had just received a new revelation and in truth, he had. "Mark," he said. "That's it. That is what is going on. It is a battle for the truth. It's just what we have been praying about. We have been praying that the TRUTH would be revealed and that people would be set free. It is no wonder I have been attacked with lies. Lies are the enemy of the truth. Not only that, but those vandals who spray painted the church are not our enemy. They are just people who have been deceived by listening to things that are untrue. The lies are the enemy, those little foxes, the Creatures of the Forest, they are the enemy. Thank you Mark!"

Together they formed a new plan to help bring new life to the prayer meetings. Obviously they were on the right track because at that same moment the creatures were fighting back.

On the other side of town there was a ministerial meeting, where most of the pastors had gathered to talk about Pastor Steve. George Bennet, as the oldest pastor in town, had called the meeting. Jealousy had been poking at his mind for weeks. He wanted to talk about both Steve and Mark. While his church had been dwindling, those two young pastors' churches were growing. Accusations of sheep stealing and suspected false doctrine were discussed but the news of Steve and Lucy seemed to be the hottest topic of the morning. The Creatures of the Forest had been whispering suspicious accusations to Pastor George. Not realizing what was happening, he had started to believe them. Not only that but he had shared his new opinions to some of the other pastors in town. This news about Steve and Lucy was just the icing on the cake. The plan to divide the pastors was working.

Jesus is Truth
He is Creature Killing Truth

Chapter 7

Whatsoever Things

Are True

Caroline woke up quite early the next morning. She wanted to have some quiet time before Steve woke up. She carried a cup of coffee, two slices of toast, and her Bible to the side porch. She loved sitting there in the early morning hours. Usually there were lots of birds and no matter what the previous day held, she found those sweet little birds refreshingly prophetic. It was like their songs came straight from the throne of God, reminding her that God was still in control.

Today more than ever, she needed those birds. The Creatures of the Forest had been working overtime on her as well. She was so angry. In her mind she understood why the people in the church had called the meeting. She also understood their concerns but she just couldn't believe how quickly doubts had been voiced against Steve. Why couldn't they just give him the benefit of the doubt? She and her husband had served that community and church for more than thirty years. Steve had grown up there. She knew all of those people and they knew her. With her thoughts in a whirlwind, she bowed her head and tried to pray. However, dark troubling questions consumed her, even Mary Scott, who had been one of her best friends for years, looked at Steve with suspicion. Why?

Fighting back tears of frustration, she opened her Bible. She had been reading her Bible systematically and this day she was reading from the book of Philippians. When she began to read in chapter four she knew that the Lord was speaking to her. Feeling a new excitement welling up inside of her spirit she read Philippians 4:8-9 and reread it several times.

"Finally, brethren, whatsoever things are true, whatsoever things *are* honest, whatsoever things *are* just, whatsoever things *are* pure, whatsoever things *are* lovely, whatsoever things *are* of good report; if *there be* any virtue, and if *there be* any praise, think on these things. Those things, which ye have both learned, and received, and heard, and seen in me, do: and the God of peace shall be with you."

Peace started to flood over her like a warm shower. Soon she knew what she had to do. She started by calling her friend Mary and explained her plan. Mary was quick to agree with Caroline and the two women put their heads together until every detail had been thought of.

Just as Caroline was hanging up her phone, Steve walked into the kitchen. He seemed happier than he had for days. "Well you look rested," she said as she gave him a hug and a kiss on his cheek.

"I am Mom," he replied. I spent a few hours with Mark yesterday. He helped me see things in a whole new light. He reminded me of a verse in Song of Solomon, about the little foxes. It was just like blinders had come off my eyes. I had been so focused on trying to justify myself that I didn't realize that this attack was bigger than me. It's an attack Mom! It's an attack on the prayer meetings and the unity we have been seeing in the churches. It's an attack on the truth. We started brainstorming and we have come to the conclusion that these little foxes, who we decided to call the Creatures of the Forest, are really the enemy. It's not the vandals who spray painted the church. It's not about the whispering and the gossip. No, Mom. It's a spiritual battle. I am not the target. It's the TRUTH that is the target."

Caroline had been listening to everything Steve was saying, smiling and nodding in agreement. She let him go on for another ten minutes and then shared what the Lord had told her this morning. The two were greatly encouraged by the plans they both had formed.

After Steve had finished his second cup of coffee and a plate of scrambled eggs, he grabbed his toast in one hand and his phone in the other. "I'm off to meet Mark, Mom. I'll call you later and let you know what time I'll be back for dinner." With that, he kissed her on the cheek and slipped out the back door.

Lurking around the corner was Roger, slumped in the front seat of his old truck. As soon as he saw Steve's Toyota pull out of the driveway, he started his pickup and pulled out of his parking spot. Following a block behind Steve he mumbled, "I'll get that preacher for stealing my wife, if it's the last thing I do!"

All night the Creatures of the Forest had had a party in Roger's mind. Thoughts of hatred and jealousy were consuming him. The little Haters were having fun as well. "You know Roger, you can't trust any of the preachers in this town. They're all alike." Mumbling those same words under his breath, he continued to follow Steve. Suddenly an idea came to his mind as he picked up his cell phone. "Hey Ben, wanna hang out tonight? I've got some ideas I want to throw around, and see what you think."

He followed Steve a few more miles and turned down a different road when Steve pulled into the driveway of Pastor Mark's house. Steve never knew he was being followed but now Mark Stewart, pastor of the little brown church on the corner, was also on Roger's list. As a matter of fact, all of the preachers in town were now his enemies. "They're all the same. They're all the same. They're all the same." Over and over the Creatures of the Forest chanted as the same words poured out of Roger's mouth.

Mark had called several of the local pastors. Not everyone responded favorably to Mark's invitation but some did and they were all waiting for Steve when he showed up. Unaware of the catastrophes about to happen to them all, they sipped on steaming mugs of coffee before coming to the business at hand.

Graycin McCoy, who everyone called Grey, was the pastor from the church on Third Street. He started the discussion. "Mark, why don't you tell us all why you called us to come this morning?"

Mark stood, thanked everyone for coming and then said, "You all know by now the slanderous rumors going around town about Steve. I myself, do not believe any of the rumors. As a matter of fact, without Steve knowing, I did a little undercover sleuthing. I talked at great length with Lucy Woodard. She is just as bewildered by the accusations as Steve is. The only time they have ever had a moment alone was last week when she came to his office to talk to Pastor Steve about her marriage troubles. Steve's secretary, Janey Fisher and the church custodian Mitchel Clarkson were there in the church building when Lucy arrived. Steve's office door was left open, as is his custom, whenever he sees a woman alone in his office. At no time were they entirely alone. Other than that, neither Steve or Lucy have any idea why these rumors have started or where they have come from. It is my belief that this is an attack on the city wide prayer meetings that we have been having. Since there is no way to establish any of these rumors as fact, I would like to say that I support Pastor Steve and I hope you will too. I am also going to ask all of my congregation to come out in support of Pastor Steve tomorrow night at the Truth prayer meeting. I'm asking that you would do the same. If we can stay united, then the Creatures of the Forest won't win."

At that last statement, everyone looked at Mark, with confusion on their faces and began mumbling to each other. Steve saw the confusion on their faces and quickly started to explain. He told them about the little foxes in Song of Solomon. Then he shared about how the lies and deceptive thoughts that were going around town, were the real enemy. He explained why he and Mark had begun to call them, the Creatures of the Forest. He told them that he wasn't looking for the person or persons responsible for the writing on his church building. He told them that he believed this whole event was a spiritual attack on the prayer meetings.

"Friends," Steve continued. "You all know how significant the prayer meetings have become. And we knew that as soon as we started praying about the Truth that the devil would be mad. I expected something to come against us but I never expected this. I was so blindsided by my own thoughts of injustice that I didn't see the real target. How can we, as leaders in the body of Christ, ever see real revival if we are divided? This attack was meant to divide us. I'm asking that all of you bring your congregation out tomorrow night and let's have the best prayer meeting yet. Surely if we cry out to God he will answer us."

Everyone was moved by what Steve and Mark had to say. They all agreed to encourage as many people as they could, to come out in support of the prayer meetings.

Replace Your Thoughts By: Praying and Speaking Truth

Chapter 8

The Panic Attack

Caroline decided it was time to speed up her efforts of reaching the women in her neighborhood. She was hoping to start on the street behind her house but there was one house, where no one ever answered the door. She had gone several times hoping someone would answer her knocking. Once again she stood outside of the little grey bungalow. She had made a batch of her famous chocolate chip cookies and was hoping the smell would entice the occupant to come to the door.

Harriet was peeking out the front window just as the widow stepped up to her door. She lingered a little longer than she intended and Caroline saw her. She had no choice but to answer the knock. She hadn't seen or talked to anyone in so long, she wasn't even sure her voice would work. "Hello," she croaked. "Can I help you?"

Caroline had stepped up to this porch door and knocked so many times and no one ever answered her that she stumbled over her words in surprise. "Ah, yes yes. Ah, I live down the street and I have been having some women over for tea. We talk and have a good time. I was wondering if you would like to come. I really think you would like it."

"Ah, no. I don't think I should go out. You see, I haven't been well." Harriet said, while starting to close the door but Caroline was not one to be dismissed so easily. She had her foot in the doorway and the door only partially closed.

"Please come. If you haven't been well, it might feel good to get out. I brought you some cookies too," she said, while pushing the plate through the crack in the doorway. "I don't mean to bother you but I would like to pray for you, especially since you haven't been well. Would that be ok?"

Harriet nodded her head without saying a word while Caroline prayed. "Lord please touch my new friend today. I don't know her needs but you know her better than I do. Please be with her. Help her to know that she isn't alone. In Jesus name, amen." Then speaking to Harriet again she said, "I would be really happy to have you come to my house. We are going to get together tomorrow afternoon about 1 pm. Would you think about it?"

Harriet agreed to think about coming but she had no intention of doing so.

Later that day a panic attack came over Harriet. Fearful thoughts attacked her while her heart began to beat double time. At first she thought she was having a heart attack, as the pain was so great that she clutched at her chest. Then as soon as it came, it went away. It had never come and gone so quickly before. She wondered what made this time different. She needed to focus, to try and think about why this had happened. "Maybe I ate something unusual today. Or maybe it wasn't something new I ate but something I didn't eat. Did I sleep more last night than other nights?" No matter how much she tried to understand, she just couldn't.

Then, suddenly without warning, another panic attack came over her but this time it was building. Stronger and stronger the attack grew and her mind began to whirl in many directions. She started to cry out but nothing would come out of her mouth. Attacks like these had become her worst nightmares.

The Creatures of the Forest had been quite unhappy about Caroline's visit. Her prayers had started to unravel their webs. The most devastating part of her prayer was the name of Jesus. These creatures had not heard that name in a long time and when they heard it, their bodies started to dissolve. There was a weakness that came over them and their wispy wings started to tear as they tried to fly away. Trying to exert their authority over Harriet, they attacked her brain with fear and caused that first panic attack. They knew they were weak but didn't realize their strength had been so seriously compromised. After Harriet recovered from her panic so quickly, they sent a message for friends to came and help.

Fear and his Fearlings had called on both Hopeless and Despair. They came with a vengeance and attacked Harriet with all their might. The Fearlings were strengthened by their presence. One by one their wings started to heal and their bodies grew stronger. The whole group pounced on Harriet and was choking the very life out of her. Spinning her thoughts faster than ever they shouted at her, "You are worthless. No one will ever love you. You will never be well. This is your life. Things will never change." Down and down and down she fell into the pit that Despair had dug for her. After what seemed like hours, her heart and mind twisted into a jumbled mess. In a stupor, she collapsed on the floor.

She never came to herself until the morning sun began to shine through her window. She stirred and stretched her aching muscles. Laying on the floor all night had left her unrested at best. She tried to shake her muddled head. Why had she slept there? What happened? Then she remembered the attack. The Creatures of the Forest had been particularly cruel to her last night. They had attacked her from every angle. Now as those memories flooded her mind, another attack threatened to overwhelm her.

Fearlings were chanting over and over to her, "Worthless! Worthless! Worthless! You can't trust anyone. Worthless! Worthless! Worthless! You're all alone. Worthless! Worthless! Worthless!"

"I've got to get out of here," she thought, as the walls of her house started to close in on her. Everywhere she turned there were creatures whispering in her ear. Louder and louder they murmured until she thought she was going to lose her mind.

Without even brushing her hair or changing the clothes she had slept in, she ran out of the house. She had no idea where she was going. It had been so long since she had walked outside that the sun was hurting her eyes. After a two minute sprint, she found herself right in front of Caroline's house. The older woman seeing her, thought Harriet had come to have tea with the other ladies. They were all arriving at the same moment and they descended on Harriet in a group of friendly hugs, leading her right into Caroline's house. She hadn't intended to come but she was obligated to stay now.

"Harriet," Caroline said. "Welcome to our tea party. I'm so glad you are here. Come sit next to me."

Caroline introduced everyone and started pouring tea. Stella had brought a plate of lemon blueberry muffins and was passing them around the room. Sarah Handler was there as well as Amy Knowles, she was the wife of the hardware shop owner. The two were chatting about the local craft fair. There were several others that were there as well and the whole room was buzzing.

After everyone had gotten their tea and muffins the room got quiet as one by one each lady shared a story telling what God had done for them that week. It seemed as if they were all taking turns as if they all had something to say. There were some who were having some very difficult problems in their lives. Harriet was surprised to hear how many of these women were suffering yet they all seemed happy. How could they be happy when they were having so many problems? The widow who invited her was sitting quietly next to her, not saying much but listening to every word. Each time someone started talking, Caroline would take notes. Harriet wasn't sure what the note taking was for but the older woman took care to write down as many details as she could. Suddenly Harriet realized everyone was looking at her.

Caroline seemed to sense Harriet's uneasiness and quickly jumped in. "Harriet, all of us here have either just gone through a difficult situation or we are in one now. We are a support group of sorts. We share things that are going on in our lives and we listen to each other. Then we pray together and ask the Lord Jesus to help us. That is why I take notes, because I want to remember what I should be praying for."

There was that name again, Jesus. Harriet was confused. Who was this

Jesus? Was he real? If so, why was he so special? Somewhere in the back of her mind she recalled her grandmother talking about Jesus. Her grandmother had died many years ago and nobody had talked about him since, except at Christmas time. Didn't he have something to do with Santa Claus?

Caroline was touching her shoulder and looking right at her. Harriet felt a bit ashamed that her mind had wandered. She hoped no one had noticed. "Harriet, would you like to share something?"

She shook her head no just as the Fearlings started to talk to her. "Run away. You don't know these people. You can't trust them. This room is too crowded. Get out now. These people are crazy." Harriet could feel the familiar panic rising in her chest. Her mind had wandered again.

"Harriet, would you like me to pray for you? You seem out of sorts." What was it Caroline had just asked her? She came to herself just as Caroline and the rest of the ladies started to pray. She knew something good had happened the last time Caroline had prayed for her but she didn't know what. Her mind was starting to spin out of control again when suddenly she heard the words, "In Jesus name, Amen!" There was that name again. As soon as they heard the name of Jesus, the Fearlings unhooked their claws from her mind and she could tell that the panic was gone. What was it about that name?

When the prayer was over, Caroline stood and said, "Ladies, God spoke to me about how we needed to do more than pray. We need to verbally declare Truth. That means, that we all need to speak, out loud, the Truth of what God says and thinks about us. We have been believing lies about ourselves and we need to speak the truth until we believe it. The Bible says that we were created in the image of God. God spoke the world with everything in it with just his words. He didn't have any dirt in his pocket. All he used was his words. If we were created in his image than our words have power too. We need to speak the truth and keep saying the truth till we believe it. You may not realize it now, but God loves you and he wants to be a part of your lives. All you have to do, to become a part of God's family, is to recognize that you are nothing without him. He wants you to believe that He loves you and that he will forgive you for all of the mistakes, sins, and bad choices you have made. He wants to be your forever friend and live inside of you. I would really like you to pray with me if you want to be a part of God's family like I am. See, I printed out a prayer we can all pray but I wanted you to read it first, so that you will know if you want to do this. On the back of this page I printed some of my favorite Bible verses that tells us what God thinks about us. I'm not trying to arm twist anyone. This has to be your choice." Finishing those words Caroline passed out the papers with a prayer printed on it.

It read, "*God, I recognize that I have not lived my life for You. I have been living for myself. I realize that I need You and I want You in my life. I believe that Your Son Jesus Christ gave His life for me on the cross at Calvary, and I want to receive the forgiveness you promised. Come into my life now. Take control of my life. Live in my heart and be my Heavenly Father, my King, my Lord, and my Savior. From this day forward, I will no longer be controlled by sin, or the desire to please myself, but I will follow You all the days of my life. I ask this in Jesus' precious name.*"

After a few minutes when Caroline thought everyone had had a chance to read the prayer and think about what it meant, she asked if anyone wanted to pray that prayer out loud with her. And almost everyone said yes, except Harriet. She seemed frozen into place and didn't even acknowledge that she had even heard what the widow had said. The ladies had been silently reading and nodding in agreement but Harriet just stared at the paper. It was as if there were no letters written on it at all. Her mind went blank and she couldn't think, let alone read. After the group prayed, Harriet was still sitting frozen in place. She couldn't process what Caroline was saying. Her eyes glazed over and she felt like she was transported to another time and place. She remembered sitting on her grandmother's lap and her grandma was singing. Singing? Yes, she remembered now, only she was singing too. What was the song they used to sing together? While the melody eluded her the words came to her mind like cool water. Yes, now I remember, "Jesus loves the little children, all the children of the world." Could it be true? She was grown now. Did Jesus still love her? She folded the paper and stuck it in her pocket. She would spend some more time thinking about this later.

Not noticing that Harriet had not participated with the rest, Caroline was ready to go on. "I'm going to start by telling you some of the things God says. I am fearfully and wonderfully made. God created me and said I was good. The Holy Spirit lives in me and he has not given me a spirit of fear but one of power, of love and a sound mind. I have the mind of Christ. Since God is for me, then no weapon formed against me can prosper."

When Caroline finished she looked at her friend Mary and nodded for her to make some Truth statements of her own. Some of the ladies were self conscious about making statements like this. They wondered if they sounded too proud to say things like that. Others just couldn't find any good words to say.

Caroline tried to explain, "I'm not making these things up. These are things that God himself has said about us. Our problem is that some of us have forgotten who we are in Christ and others don't even know what God thinks about us. We are his daughters and he is proud of us. I want all of you to spend some time this week to reflect on what God says about you. You see, what God says about us is Truth. The problem is that we believe the lies of the devil. His lies tell us that we are useless, unloved, and rejected but that isn't the Truth. The Truth is about who God is and what He says about us.

After Caroline encouraged the rest of the ladies to make Truth statements, a few more tried to come up with something to say. When each one finished, Caroline would add to what they said, then she hugged each one and looked them directly in their eyes saying, "You are a mighty woman of God." Wrapping everything up she said, "Ladies, when you get home, open up the Bibles that I gave you last week and see if you can find a new Truth to say to yourself. Bring those Truths with you next week. We will share them and speak those words over each other. With those final words the widow picked up another Bible that she had sitting on the table next to her and handed it to Harriet. "I believe this will be a comfort to you, my dear. Read it. If you have any questions you can come talk to me whenever you like."

There was more tea and cookies, along with lots of friendly conversation. Harriet had never been in a meeting like this before. She didn't really know how to process it all. She had just started to leave when several of the women her age surrounded her, asking if she would like to go to lunch with them sometime. Stella invited her to go to church with her Sunday morning and several others asked for her phone number. What had she gotten herself into?

CREATURES OF THE FOREST

Jesus is Truth
He is Creature Killing Truth

Chapter 9

The Creature's Plan

Roger made it to Ben's house a little later than he had planned. He stopped off at the library to checkout some books on explosives. He had never been a violent man but lately his mind was consumed with so much hatred that he could barely focus and violence seemed to be his only outlet. Roger didn't even recognize himself anymore. He didn't know, that because he hadn't taken those thoughts captive, they had captured him. He wasn't thinking straight. He wondered how he had changed so suddenly when in fact it had been a gradual transition every time he believed a lie.

Armed with an arm full of books and a couple of six packs of beer, he knocked on Ben's door. Someone Roger didn't even know answered the door. It was a friend of Ben's with one of the girls from the camping trip. Mandy, the girl Roger liked was there as well. There was the skunky herbal odor of marijuana coming from the living room and when Roger looked towards the living room, he could see the room was full of smoke. Roger had never smoked anything before, even cigarettes, but in his current frame of mind and the Creatures of the Forest telling him it was a good thing to do, he jumped in with both feet.

A couple of hours later, after most everyone was gone, Roger and Ben sat at the kitchen table. Ben had always been a little unstable and it didn't take Roger long to talk him into what he wanted to do. Both of their minds were so clouded by the beer and marijuana that there was no more restraint. What they were about to do would bring all of those hypocrites to their knees. How dare they preach about God and love when they were all thieves and adulterers.

On the table was a detailed plan. They would strike two churches at the same time. If they could destroy some church buildings and make people afraid to participate in church events, maybe they could save other guy's wives from being lured away from their husbands. They realized that they might kill a few hypocritical Christians at the same time but by now, all reason was gone. If this plan worked they would blow up two more next week. Of course the first church to go had to be Pastor Steve's and they would take out Pastor Mark's church too. After a few more drinks the plan was made and with it a new shopping list. In his haste, Roger had miscalculated. He would need a whole lot more stuff.

The Creatures of the Forest were quite proud of their plan. They were going to take out anyone and everyone who stood for truth. Since Roger had based all of these plans on a lie, their plan seemed perfect. He was their guy and they were pretty proud of him. Laughing, they buzzed around and around in Roger's mind. They had him right where they wanted him. Soon no one in town would be praying for Truth any more. They would be praying that the vengeance would end. The fact that innocent people would be hurt or killed mattered not to Roger and Ben. As a matter of fact the more that died the better. They would teach this town a lesson.

Replace Your Thoughts By: Praying and Speaking Truth

Chapter 10

Hidden Battles

Caroline was so happy that Harriet had come for tea. She was concerned that something had happened to her, to make the young woman arrive in such haste. Her clothes had been all crumpled and she looked like she hadn't brushed her hair in weeks. "I have to follow up with her," she thought. Picking up the phone she was pleased when Harriet answered on the second ring.

"Hi Harriet, I was so happy you could come to my house today. I was wondering, did anyone invite you to church this Sunday? Oh she did? Well that's nice, I'm glad Stella invited you. I wanted to invite you for lunch after church. I plan to make lasagna and it is more than enough for just my son and myself. If you would like to come, I'll invite Stella too."

Harriet had planned to call Stella when she got home and excuse herself from the church invitation but she was too late. The Creatures of the Forest had been fighting in her mind and causing a great deal of confusion. They had gotten her mind so muddled that she had forgotten to call. Now it looked like she was going to church Sunday morning and to lunch.

The Creatures that plagued her were unhappy that she had gone to Caroline's house but they realized they had to be a bit more subtle. Their hasty actions that morning had caused her to run right into that prayer meeting. Well that wouldn't happen again. Not if they could help it. Now with Sunday morning looming in the forecast, they called a meeting to come up with a plan.

Caroline was busy with a plan of her own. "Stella, I'm so glad you invited Harriet to church Sunday. I'm worried she will back out and not go. Would you be willing to go over to her house tomorrow? Let's see if she will go out for lunch with us."

So it was planned. They would meet at Caroline's house at 11am, pray together and then visit Harriet.

Harriet woke up the next day much later but happier than she had been in a long time. Maybe there was something about this Jesus. She washed and blow dried her hair and then fixed a pot of coffee. While the coffee dripped into her carafe, she got dressed. She had just poured a cup and had taken two sips when her doorbell rang. It was Caroline and Stella. She really didn't want to let them in, her house was a mess and she was sure it smelled bad too. She had forgotten to take out the garbage last week. But they had been so nice to her the day before that she couldn't ignore them.

Once inside, the two visitors told her of their plans. They wanted to treat her to lunch. She hadn't been out for lunch in months. As a matter of fact it had been months since she had done anything special with her hair. Thank goodness she had washed it before they came. Twenty minutes later she was sitting in the front passenger seat of Stella's car. She had been totally unprepared for this outing but she was finding it to be quite enjoyable. After lunch the three new friends decided to visit a few antique shops and finished in the local coffee shop. By the time they drank their last cups of coffee, the sun was starting to set.
There was something special about these two ladies. Whenever Harriet was with them, the Creatures of the Forest had to stay quiet. They tried, several times, to interfere with Harriet 's mind. They could tell this outing wasn't good. It even caused some arguments among the Fearlings. Some said they should call for Despair to come. Others said Harriet belonged to them and they didn't want to share. Thankfully, she was blissfully unaware of the debate.

ෆෆෆෆෆෆෆෆෆෆෆෆෆෆෆෆ

Caroline dropped Harriet off at her house and it was dark in the living room when she entered. Shadows cast an eerie darkness in the corners. Little did Harriet know she was walking into a trap. Memories of her attacker flooded her mind. Fear was attacking with all of his might. "Someone is here. Look in that corner. See? You're alone with no one to help you. You never should have left the house. Now someone is here and you will never escape. Never escape! Never escape!"

Harriet's mind began to spin. How could she be so foolish as to leave her house. "It was a foolish thing to do, leaving the house. It wasn't safe. It wasn't safe. Never do that again. I'll never do that again. It isn't safe. I have no safe place. Where can I go? No I can't go outside..."

With her heart beating faster and faster she spun around the room looking in every corner. After the living room, she entered the rest of the house checking every closet and under all of the beds. Finally after she was certain no one was there, she plopped down on her couch and dissolved into tears. "I can't go on living this way," she thought. Feeling completely exhausted after so much emotion, she fell into a fitful sleep. About midnight she awoke and realized she had fallen asleep completely dressed, curled up on the couch. Her back ached and her eyes smarted from crying. Shuffling to the bathroom she heard a noise just outside her window. "What was that?" She wondered. Then another sound and then another. Each more scary than the one before. The Fearlings were having fun dropping pinecones on Harriet's roof. They knew just the reaction they could get. She was so afraid and yet one word kept coming to her mind.

"Jesus!" she cried. "Help me!"

She didn't really know what to expect but it was the only thing she could think of. She glanced in all directions, avoiding the windows while walking to her room. Then saying the name of Jesus again, she dropped into bed once again and fell fast asleep.

Jesus is Truth
He is Creature Killing Truth

Chapter 11

Arriving At A Dead End

Brooks Glen was a sleepy little city. Nothing much ever happened there. Once in a while someone's kid would get caught shoplifting. And there was a speed trap that often caught a few speeding out of town drivers. Other than that, little happened there. Roger felt pretty certain that his plans would get the attention of everyone. He had never amounted to much in high school. His grades were passing but nothing to be proud of. He was never accepted by the 'in crowd' and he didn't excel in sports. For once in his life, Roger would get attention. The eyes of the whole city would be on him.

Pride had joined the Creatures. "You deserve the attention Roger," he purred.
After another night of drinking and smoking pot, Roger and Ben decided that it would be better to string the church bombing along. Why bomb two or even three churches at once when it would be more effective one church at a time. Soon the whole town would be paralyzed with fear. Yes Roger would get their attention this time and those preachers would get what they deserved.

The Creatures of the Forest were spinning Roger's mind in all directions. Every moment in his past was amplified. Every slight, every unkind word, every injustice was brought to the forefront of his memory. "Unfair! Unfair! Unfair," the Creatures shouted. The darkness of the Forest was flooding his mind. Over and over they chanted, like a witches spell they consumed his thoughts.

Without any thought at all Roger staggered out of Ben's house. Ben had had plenty to drink and he was passed out on his couch. Roger, on the other hand, was wide awake. The Creatures wouldn't let him sleep. No longer in control of his thoughts or his actions, he paused only long enough to grab a fishing knife and the spray paint from Ben's garage. He was in a hurry. The sun would be up soon and he had a lot to do before that happened.

The little brown church was the closest to Ben's house. He parked about a block away and walked to the church. On the right side was the parsonage where Mark and his family lived. Slashing all four tires of Mark's car with the fishing knife, he then took out his spray paint. At first he thought to just randomly spray the car but the Creatures had another idea. As if unseen hands held the cans of paint he wrote:

> I know who you are
> Hypocrite
> You'll get what's coming to you!

Leaving Mark's church he drove to the church on third street. There was an apartment in the back, attached to the church. This was where Grey lived with his wife and small daughter. Two cars were parked next to the apartment. Roger slashed the tires on both of them. Then taking his spray paint, he wrote the same message on both cars.

Looking up and down the street as he left, he saw the oldest church in the city just two blocks away. This will get attention he thought. Leaving his car in the middle of the street with the driver's door open he walked up to the stained glass windows. Large and stately the windows had stood guardian over the church for over one hundred and twenty years. He paused as if contemplating whether he should do it or not. The Creatures started screaming in his mind, "Do it! Do it! Do it! Hurry up before someone sees you. The sun is about to rise. Do it! Do it! Do it!" Overwhelmed by the thoughts and unable to resist, he lifted the spray can and started to write:

> This is
> Jut the
> Biginning

By now his mind was so muddled he couldn't spell right and could hardly hold the can as he wrote. With all self control lost he grabbed some rocks from the flower beds and threw them at the windows. The stained glass resisted the smaller rocks so he grabbed some paving bricks that lined the walkway. One by one he threw them, shattering over a hundred years of beauty. Then he staggered back to his truck and drove about two blocks away. He had grown up in this town but at that moment he was lost. He didn't know where he lived and he didn't know how to get there. He had given away his soul and his mind to the Creatures of the Forest. Roger didn't exist at that moment. Hatred existed in Roger's mind and he was in control now. From this moment on, he and his friends would tell Roger what to do. The truck slowly came to a stop near to the end of a dead end street. A fitting place for Roger as he was quickly arriving at the dead end of his life. Somehow he parked his truck and turned off the engine. Tipping to one side he passed out, while the darkness of the Forest covered him like a blanket.

The next morning, Roger found himself scrunched up in the front seat of his truck. He rubbed his eyes and tried to remember why he was parked in such a strange place. He remembered some of his actions from the night before but the rest was only a blur.

Replace Your Thoughts By: Praying and Speaking Truth

Chapter 12

The Prayer of

Agreement

Steve was on the porch having coffee with his mom when the phone rang. He stood up to answer when his mom said, "No I'll get it. I was going to get us some more coffee anyways."

Caroline grabbed the phone on her way to the kitchen. "Hello!"

When Steve saw the look of shock on her face, he jumped up to stand by her side. "What is it Mom?"

An hour later Steve was at Mark's house, along with Grey, and Bishop Wallace, the pastor of the oldest church with the stained glass windows. The police were there as well and they were all asking or answering questions. Unfortunately, once again there were more questions than answers. No one had any idea who was responsible for the vandalism on the stately old church and the pastors' cars. Only now they knew it wasn't just Steve who was being targeted. As much as the pastors wanted to appear strong and full of faith, they were battling their own Creatures of the Forest. Mark and Grey were slowly being consumed by Fear. He had been methodically planting fearful thoughts into each man's mind. What does this mean? Is my family at risk? What about my little daughter? What should we do? What can we do?

When the police were finished asking questions and stood to leave, Bishop Wallace held up his meaty hand and asked them to wait a few minutes. At six foot, four inches tall, he was a massive man, who few ever argued with. The police sat down and the Bishop stood up. With a pleasant southern drawl, he began to speak. "Have we all forgotten, gentlemen? That our battle is not with flesh and blood? We are fighting principalities and powers. This isn't an attack on us, brothers. It's against the Lord. (This he said drawing out each letter of the word Lord). Detective, please would you and your men stay and join us for a few minutes of prayer?" It wasn't really a question as much as it was an order. No one argued with the Bishop.

With everyone standing, Bishop Wallace started to pray, his deep voice reverberating throughout the room. "Lord, in Jesus name we stand here in agreement. Your word says that if two or more of us agree in prayer that you are there. We acknowledge your presence and we have come to ask that you would give us wisdom. You told us in your word that if we needed wisdom that you would give it to us. Tell us what to do, Lord. We need direction. These fine policemen need your help. Obviously whoever is behind these threats needs prayer too. Lord save his soul. He must be tormented in his mind. We come against the evil thoughts that he is fighting. There is no one too far gone that you cannot save. So we're praying for him right now. Thank you for your protection and your guidance. Thank you for your peace. We need a touch of that right now Lord. Some of us are scared and fearful for our congregations and our families. So what we need is your peace and guidance. We ask this all in Jesus Name, Amen."

A holy hush came over them all and peace flooded their hearts. Even the policemen were touched. The detective wiped tears from his face as he left the room.

After the police were gone, the four men looked at each other and without a word, got down on their knees and poured their hearts out to the Lord. They weren't afraid anymore but they could sense that something bigger was coming. After an emotional hour of prayer, they stood. A couple of them were teary eyed but they all had a determined look on their face. They were ready. They didn't know what they were ready for, but they were ready.

Steve broke the silence, "While I was praying, the Lord spoke to my heart that we should increase our prayer meetings for Truth. Would you guys encourage your congregations to come? Better yet, would any of you be willing to host some of the meetings in your church? I believe this attack is the result of these prayer meetings. Jesus said he is the Truth and he also said that the truth would set us free. We need freedom, brothers and the only way to get freedom is through Truth. This city needs the Truth. Also, we need to do more than pray. We need to speak the Truth out loud. Abraham believed God for things as though they were. Too often we speak things we see and wish they were not! We need to speak Truth. We need to gather all of the churches. We need to stand in unity against these attacks because something bigger than us is going on."

"So how should we go about this?" Grey asked.

"Let's make a plan. If every church in town, is willing to host a prayer meeting, then we could have two full weeks of daily prayer, twice at each church. Then after those two weeks, we can go someplace. I think the baseball field would be big enough. We could encourage people to bring lawn chairs and snacks so that they could spend the whole day. We could have people designated to read scripture, out loud, especially the ones which state who we are in Christ. We could have special prayer times where people could pray for each other. I believe that if we can do this and be united, God will hear us and answer our prayers. I believe we can silence the Creatures of the Forest.

So armed with pens and paper the four pastors began to make plans.

C33CSCSCSCSCSCSCSCSCSCSCSCSCS

Caroline, Stella, and Sarah had a late lunch later that same day. Caroline had called her two friends and asked them if they could get together. They needed to do some brainstorming. It seemed like the devil was attacking on every side. Caroline had a plan that she felt certain would seriously diminish the effect of his lies but she needed help.

After the ladies had finished their lunch and between sips of tea, Caroline began to explain her ideas. "I've been praying a lot about the situation here in our small city. At first I didn't know what I could do to help, if anything. Then I remembered what Jesus said in Matthew 18:18-20. He said that we have the power to loose things here on earth and that when we do this it would be established in Heaven. He also said that if we have unity and agree when we pray that he would hear us and give us what we ask for. I want to loose warring angels to defeat the Creatures of the Forest. If we agree, it will be done. I believe we need to be proactive."

Then Caroline began to read what Jesus said, "Verily I say unto you, Whatsoever ye shall bind on earth shall be bound in heaven: and whatsoever ye shall loose on earth shall be loosed in heaven. Again I say unto you, That if two of you shall agree on earth as touching anything that they shall ask, it shall be done for them of my Father which is in heaven. For where two or three are gathered together in my name, there am I in the midst of them."

Sarah was nodding her head vigorously while Caroline spoke. She responded, "That's right. I was reading in 2 Corinthians 10:5, just last night. It said, 'casting down imaginations, and every high thing that exalteth itself against the knowledge of God, and bringing into captivity every thought to the obedience of Christ.' We need to teach people how to bring their thoughts under control. God wouldn't tell us to do this if it weren't possible."

"Is it possible? How do we teach people to control their thoughts?" asked Stella. I have trouble myself dealing with my thought life. I worry all of the time about my kids and how I'm going to pay my bills. My own thoughts are out of control. How can I teach someone if I can't do it myself?"

"Those are fair questions, Stella." Caroline answered. "I have given this much thought and I believe God has shown me some effective ways to control our thoughts. First, we need to be careful what we put in our minds. That includes both positive things and negative things. Everything we put in our mind has an effect on us. I want each of us to give some thought as to what we think about. Then write it down. If the thoughts are destructive then next to each of those thoughts, write down a scripture verse that answers those thoughts. God has an answer for every thought. For example Stella, you said you worry about your kids. Write that down then let's search the Word of God for scriptures that can replace those worries. We can help each other."

"Here's a Bible verse." said Sarah. "Psalms 127:3 says that children *are* a heritage of the LORD. This means that our kids are something special to God. He gave them to us to bless us. If they are a blessing, then that is what we should say about them. My son is a blessing from the Lord. He is blessed and he will be everything God wants him to be. I don't have to worry because God holds my son's life in his hands. God loves him more than I do and therefore, I have nothing to be afraid of."

Caroline smiled, "This is going to be better than I thought. We can make up whole lists of Bible verses to change our thought life. Of course it won't change how we think overnight. We have to go to war with our thoughts. We have to force ourselves to think differently. We all have so many negative things deeply ingrained in us that these dark Creatures will not let go easily. I've been missing my husband so much since he died, I'm going to start replacing my own sad thoughts with God's word."

"How about the three of us put together some Creature Killing scriptures and bring them tomorrow afternoon for our tea." Caroline continued. "I'll explain everything to the ladies when they get here. You know the Bible says the Truth will set us free. Well, it's time we started believing the Truth and not the lies. There are so many things happening in town that we have a responsibility to do what we can do. For me, I choose to believe the Truth and not the lies from the Creatures of the Forest. I'm going to own the Truth, make it mine. I believe this will make a difference."

Jesus is Truth
He is Creature Killing Truth

Chapter 13

The First Night

The first of the fourteen prayer meetings was scheduled to start in two days. Pastor Grey's church would be the first to host the meetings. Since that would be a Monday night, the pastors would have an opportunity to announce it to their congregations on Sunday. They had also taken out advertisements on the radio and the newspaper.

Roger heard about the meetings while he listened to the radio in his shop. The first thing he did was call Ben. "Hey buddy, did you hear that those preachers are planning more prayer meetings? This will work great for us. We'll be able to practice our explosives. Do you think we can have something ready for Monday night?"

Ben was just as excited as Roger was. The Creatures of the Forest had been tormenting him for days. His father had been a cruel man. Growing up had been a nightmare. Many nights he and his brother Sam, went to bed beaten and hungry. His mom would often beg Ben and his brother to forgive their father. The old man beat her too and she always forgave him, even after he broke her arm and punched her in the eye. She used to tell her boys that it was the Christian thing to do. Ben decided he would never forgive his dad and if that meant he wasn't being Christian then, so be it. The old man didn't deserve forgiveness. When Sam couldn't take any more, he left home and went to Alaska. Those memories started flooding back into Ben's mind. Lately they came in the form of nightmares. Over and over the Creatures of Darkness reminded him of his hatred for his father. Every morning he awoke in a sweat with his bedsheets rumpled and damp. No, he would never forgive. Unforgiveness turned to hatred and soon Hatred was consuming his mind. His mom was weak. She turned to religion and that made her weak. The more Ben thought about it, a storm began to brew in his mind. He hated his dad for abusing him. He hated Sam for leaving him. He hated his mom for forgiving his dad. He hated Christians for teaching his mom to forgive.

As soon as he hung up the phone with Roger, Ben started making a list. He would be ready when Roger came over tonight. There was an unholy excitement brewing in his mind. He couldn't wait to see one of those churches go up in flames.

After work that night Roger and Ben drove an hour away to buy supplies. They didn't want to take the chance that the local stores would have surveillance cameras. Their plan wouldn't work if they were caught before their grand finale.

Having read several articles on the internet about improvised explosive devices, they started shopping. The cost of the materials was staggering. They decided they would have to do some additional improvising of their own. Cutting back on several of the items listed on the web, they paid with a credit card and drove back to Ben's house.

Working all day Sunday, till late at night, they figured they were ready for the first meeting. As soon as they finished, they drove around the church. They were hoping to get their homemade bomb in place before the sun came up and before anyone saw them. There were dogs barking and skunks loitering around garbage cans. For over an hour they sat in Roger's truck, wondering if they would have to wait till the next night. But then things seemed to quiet down. The two of them started walking around the church building trying to figure out where the best place would be to place the bomb, cursing under their breath for having not thought about this before. They had no idea what they were doing. Deception was twisting their brains to such a point that they began to believe that it wouldn't matter where they put it as long as it was attached to the church and it blew up.

They found a place under some bushes between one of the sanctuary windows and the front door. Their plan was to set off the bomb with a cheap cell phone that Ben had purchased years before. So they set their makeshift bomb under the bushes and attached it to the center of the bush using some twine. They took great care that their bomb was nestled deep under the bush and even hollowed out a place in the dirt so it could be covered over and not be seen. Fluffing up the grass as they left the spot, they were confident that this would go off without any problems.

Monday morning, storm clouds covered the sky. The weather had taken an unexpected turn and thunderstorms with high winds were forecasted. Many people had been excited and involved with the preparations for the two weeks of prayer, however, Frustration, a dark little creature was working double time to cause the workers to give up. He was sure the bad weather would encourage people to stay home. So he took advantage of the situation and twisted the thoughts of any who would listen. "Don't bother volunteering today. No one is coming anyways. Just look at the weather. Stay home. You don't need to go tonight." Over and over he spread his web. Joined with Doubt and Fear they roamed from person to person. As the storm clouds covered the sky so did the darkness of the Forest darken anyone who would listen.

Discouragement had been whispering in Grey's ear all morning. He had such high hopes for this first meeting, that when the unexpected weather loomed on the horizon he almost gave up. Calling Steve on the phone he questioned if they should cancel this first meeting. His volunteers were dwindling in number and he wasn't sure if his church facility could be ready in time. He had planned snacks and coffee for fellowship after. Now, imagining all of the things that could go wrong, he finished by saying, "We had better call the radio station and make a public service announcement, telling people not to come out tonight. The weather is getting worse by the minute and we're just not ready."

Steve sensed the work of the two cousins Frustration and Quit. "Grey, listen to yourself. Do you even hear what you are saying? How can we quit now? These problems will work themselves out. It doesn't matter if your church is cleaned up perfectly. It doesn't matter if we have enough snacks for the fellowship after. As a matter of fact we don't need anything. We just need to open the doors and let people come in. The Holy Spirit will do the rest. I have a feeling that we just have to push through all of these problems."

Outside, battle lines were being drawn and like Goliath of old, the enemy's only weapon was his ability to speak. The Creatures of the Forest were calling on every friend they could muster. Fear was actually working himself up in a frenzy. "We're going to die. We'll all die. This is bad. Oh yes this is bad." He was so stressed out that his Forest buddies didn't feel that he could handle the stress. They were sure that any minute he would fall apart and disappear in a puff of smoke. Their only hope was that he would be able to take a few people down with him when he went.

Unfortunately, these Creatures had reproduced to such an extent that their numbers were staggering. If Steve and his friends could see the battle with their natural eyes they would have been terrified. They knew that the weapons of this warfare were indeed powerful. They had faith. They had unity but did they truly possess the power that was needed to fight this battle?

By 6 pm Grey and several other pastors huddled under umbrellas waiting for people to begin to arrive. By 6:15 pm, Caroline and a carload of her friends pulled up to the door, however no one else came. By 7:05 pm, Grey was sure the whole event was ruined and that no one else would come. Mark and Steve walked into the church leaving Grey outside to assist anyone arriving late. The rain had not let up and everyone's cell phone was beeping with flash flood warnings. Caroline was beginning to wonder if she and Steve would be able to cross the small bridge to their area of town, when it was time for them to go home. Her friends had worried looks on their faces as well. One more carload of ladies from Pastor Grey's church arrived and he escorted them inside while passing out paper towels to help them dry off.

No one was praying. The wind began to blow harder and harder. Tree branches were whipping in the wind and several had broken off. Hail began to pelt the windows and the electricity flickered on and off. Fear, enjoying the show, was walking around each one as they stood huddled in the back of the church. No one had even sat down, as Fear wound his web of pessimism around them. "This is bad. This is bad. Go home. Go home NOW! This is bad."

Angelic warriors had been on guard, watching as if disinterested yet ready for battle, with their swords drawn for action. Then suddenly the rain stopped and the wind died down. Everyone looked at each other in the silence as if the spell had been broken. Steve was the first to speak. "I don't know what just happened but somehow God did a miracle." Little did they know the battle that had been won that night in the little city of Brooks Glen.

God had watched Roger and Ben the night before while they laid their trap, just outside the front door of the church. With a flick of his wrist, the wind began to blow to do his bidding. There was no need for battle as the storm clouds began to gather in response to the Heavenly Conductor. Over the unsuspecting city they hovered while the storm began to gain strength. The storm that threatened that first night of prayer was the hand of God. Raining until the ground was saturated, the improvised plans that Roger and Ben had so carelessly laid out were soaked and worthless. No matter how many times they tried to activate the bomb, the call never went through to do its bidding.

The Creatures of the Forest were angry. Whose fault was it anyways? Accusing each other, they began to fight, tearing each other apart. Where did that rain storm come from? There had been no battle. The whole plan was spoiled from the beginning. The bomb had been poorly made and had quickly become useless in the storm. Anger was quickly gaining strength until both Roger and Ben saw Murder in each other's eyes. They needed to come up with another plan and quickly. There was another prayer meeting tomorrow night.

ભ ભ ભ ભ ભ ભ ભ ભ ભ ભ ભ ભ ભ ભ ભ ભ ભ

Morning came too early for Roger. The night before had gone later than he had planned. He had to work on two cars before he could take care of his shopping list. Both he and Ben had agreed that it would be better to drive out of town to get more supplies. They had made a mess of their earlier plans and now they had to start over. No use in showing their hand or giving any local busybodies something to talk about. If they were going to succeed in their plans they had to keep their purchases a secret. They each had their shopping list and they were traveling in two different directions.

Roger didn't get on the road till after 3 pm. He was quite frustrated. He had wanted to be back to Ben's house by 6 pm. He had a lot to do if he was going to be ready for their next attack. He grabbed several items on his list at the local Wal-Mart and then drove across town for the Home Depot. By the time he was done there, the sun was starting to set and he realized that he hadn't eaten a thing since breakfast. Driving up to a fast food window, he barked out his order and waited impatiently for it to arrive. Not bothering to look, he pulled out of the parking lot and right into the side of a new Chevy Cruze. The little old lady driving the car, cast a fearful look his way when he started shaking his fist at her. Screaming obscenities out the window at the poor woman, he never even stopped, just backed up a bit, turned around and drove off. So much for not attracting attention. Yes the Creatures of the Forest were having quite a day with Roger.

Mark's church was hosting the prayer meeting that night, however it was 7:30 pm when Roger arrived at Ben's house. They had lost their opportunity to attack Mark's church so they were working on plans to attack Pastor Steve's church the next night. Ben had been laying out all of the stuff he had collected. Since their first attempt at bomb making had been a failure, they were afraid of making a lot more mistakes. Ben was fidgety and Roger was angry. Not a good combination. Fear had been playing mind games with Ben. He longed for a drink, thinking it would calm his frazzled nerves but Roger insisted that they not drink while building their bombs. It wasn't long before they were in a fist fight and Ben's lifeless body was slumped over on the floor.

The Creatures were screaming inside of Roger's head. Some were congratulating him in ridding himself of the whiny Ben. Others were accusing him, calling him an idiot and a fool. What should he do now? Dragging the body out of sight he started thinking about a simpler plan. All of his previous plans were now ruined. He needed two people to make his original plan work. Looking over his supplies, he decided he would burn the churches one by one. It would just be easier that way. Even though Steve's church was scheduled for Wednesday's prayer meeting, he would have to choose a closer church than Pastor Steve's for his first fire. It wouldn't make sense for Roger to drive all the way across town just to burn down a church. Not when there was a perfectly good one close by. Of course Roger's thoughts were irrational. But those were the only thoughts he had these days. He would set a fire in Mark's church and leave Ben's body, with his hand clutching a gas can, inside. It would look like Ben was the arsonist and had died in the process of burning down the church.

He waited till about 2 am. He wanted it to be the darkest time of night, when fewer people were around to see him. He planned to check out all the churches tomorrow afternoon on his lunch break but now he had to figure out this one in the dark. The building was on a corner, with a small driveway going around back connecting to the parsonage. Roger was afraid to drive down the little driveway for fear it would awaken the family in the parsonage but going in one of the front doors wasn't a good idea either. His head was pounding and his heart was racing. He wasn't afraid but adrenaline was pumping through his body so much that he was shaking from the excitement. Death had now become his friend. He didn't realize what a cocktail of Creatures he now had. No longer in his right mind he was serving other spirits and they were raging inside of him. They didn't care about Roger at all. Their whole purpose was to stop the Truth prayer meetings. When they were done with Roger, they would dump him as easily as he was dumping Ben tonight.

He decided to park a block away and walk back to the church. He started by checking every door and window. He got lucky when he found the door to the kitchen unlocked. Someone must have forgotten to lock it. Thinking the kitchen was a good place to set a fire, Roger walked back to his car. Casting caution to the wind, he turned off his lights and slowly drove around back. Ben was a smaller man and Roger was pretty tough from his years of auto repair. Hauling Ben, compared to truck engines was a breeze. He wasn't even out of breath. He bumped into some chairs and almost tipped over a coffee machine as he stumbled in the dark. After his eyes adjusted, he was a bit more careful when he walked. Cardboard boxes from a recent food outreach lined one of the walls. He piled them on top of each other and laying Ben's lifeless body on top, he struck a match. The first box was a bit wet and the fire fizzled. Roger snooped around the kitchen till he found some towels and cleaning supplies. Piling them all together, in one big heap, he struck a match and this time the fire caught a draft and started to burn. In his haste he forgot to position Ben's body the way he wanted but no matter, the deed was done and all he wanted to do was to get out of there.

03 03 03 03 03 03 03 03 03 03 03 03 03 03 03

Mark didn't usually have trouble sleeping but this night he tossed and turned. About 2:30 am, he decided he should just get up and spend some time praying. It seemed like the Lord often would wake him up if someone needed prayer, so thinking this was the case he padded down the steps into his kitchen to fix a cup of peppermint tea before he started to pray. He was standing in front of his kitchen window when he saw a strange glow coming through the church windows. He squinted his eyes and took a closer look. Fire! The church was on fire. He grabbed the house phone and dialed 911.

The firemen took less than ten minutes to arrive. Thanks to their quick response and the church sprinkler system, the damage was contained to the kitchen. Mark and his wife Joy were standing in the doorway when the Fire Chief called one of the local police to come and take a look at something. Mark and Joy started to follow and the Fire Chief told Joy to stay behind. It didn't take long for the three men to understand what they saw. Someone's charred body lay in a heap of ashes.

As Mark stood in the twilight hours, he pondered over the events of that evening. The Truth prayer meeting had been well attended that night, with more than enough people to make up for the poor turnout the night before. All of the churches were represented and the time of prayer had been very emotional. People were crying before the Lord asking him to reveal his Truth to them. Many came with lists of prayer requests including children who were in trouble, financial difficulties or broken marriages. The Holy Spirit spoke words of wisdom to hearts and gave peace where it was needed. It was a powerful time of prayer. Truth was found in the worship songs, the scripture reading and the fellowship afterwards. Many people were truly set free. No wonder the Creatures of the Forest were angry.

CREATURES OF THE FOREST

Replace Your Thoughts By: Praying and Speaking Truth

Chapter 14

Joy's Plan

Mark turned from the crowd huddled around his church and taking Joy by the hand walked her back to their house. Once inside he called Steve. "Steve, can you call Grey and Bishop Wallace and come right over?" He quickly told Steve about the fire. When he was finished, he told Joy that he wanted her to pack a bag and go stay at her mom's house for a couple of days.

Joy, shook her head no and said, "Did you forget the words I said on the day I married you? For better for worse, in sickness or in health, no matter what I would remain at your side? I meant those words Mark and I have a job to do. While you were talking to the Fire Chief, I was asking the Lord what he wanted me to do. I believe he spoke to me. So, I'm going over to Steve's house later this morning and have a talk with Caroline." With those words, she tipped her chin up to Mark and kissed him on the cheek. "Now, I'm going back to bed. I have work to do when the sun comes up."

Watching Joy as she turned towards the stairs, Mark couldn't help but chuckle at his spunky wife. She surely was a joy in his life. What would he do without her? Then he turned and walked back outside to the chaos that was gathered around the kitchen door of his church. There was no going back to bed for him. It wasn't long before his friends showed up. They gathered around his kitchen table while he began to tell everything he knew. There had been no word yet as to who had died in the fire or why he was there. The police weren't giving any information so it all remained a mystery. One thing for sure. The Creatures of the Forest were looking for a fight.

cs cs cs cs cs cs cs cs cs cs cs cs cs cs cs cs

Later that morning, after taking the last bite of his Double Burger with cheese, Bishop Wallace lifted his meaty hand, "Brothers, we stood just a few hundred feet from here only a few hours ago. We saw God move and I could sense his Awesome power. This is not a time to be afraid. We need to stand strong. I heard the Lord say to me, as I walked into your house Mark, that the battle is not for the weak or the feeble but for those of courage. Joshua was just a young man when Moses died. Several times the Lord spoke to him and told him to be of good courage. Brothers, this is a good fight! The Bible says to fight the good fight of faith. What value would Truth have if it didn't instill courage and faith. I believe," at this point the giant man stood and his voice began to take on an authority that would have caused lesser men to shudder. "I believe," he repeated while he slapped his hand on Mark's kitchen table for emphasis, "That God Almighty is in the Fight. If God is for us who can be against us? We are going to win this battle. It's evident in the strength of the opposition that has come against us. I choose to stand strong." With those words the other three men stood and standing shoulder to shoulder, they all declared that they would stand strong.

This night the prayer meeting would be at the Bishop's church. If there was going to be an attack, then they would be ready.

cs cs cs cs cs cs cs cs cs cs cs cs cs cs cs cs

A couple of hours later, Joy called Caroline and invited herself to the widow's house. Caroline met her at the door with the aroma of fresh coffee and cinnamon rolls. After some small talk, Joy began to tell Caroline about the fire at the church. "Mrs. Foster, you are much wiser than I am. You served along with your husband in your church for many years. You stand with Steve in his ministry even now. What do you think about all that is happening? Have you ever seen a time like right now, where the churches are under such an attack? Mark wants me to go stay at my mom's house but I believe my place is standing with him during this trying time. I believe God has a job for me to do but I don't know what that job is. God told me to come see you today. What do you think?"

Caroline, sitting in her favorite recliner, smiled, and then reached across her coffee table to take Joy's hand. "I've been in prayer this morning and I too have a job to do. I think it's great that the churches are coming together and praying but there seems to be something missing. When all these things started happening, I started to have an idea. The Lord showed me that we need to speak the Truth and I have been trying to teach some of my friends how to do that. You know Truth can and will set us free but only if we make that Truth our own. It isn't enough to just think about Truth. We have to own the Truth. Then just this morning during my quiet time, it seemed even clearer. What we need is worship. It's good to pray, it's good to declare the Truth, but we need to also worship God and thank him for the Truth he brings into our lives. We need to thank him because He is the Truth. I believe worship is the next key. If we can gather a group of people from all of the churches to add worship to the prayer I believe we will break the powers of these demonic forces that are coming against us.

Joy's eyes were bright with tears as she listened to the older woman. She closed her eyes for a moment and paused before she began to speak. "I knew I was supposed to come see you. My sister and I used to sing together. I played the guitar and she an electric keyboard. We had many opportunities to use our music for the Lord. Last year, she died giving birth to my nephew. I was so crushed that I haven't picked up my guitar since. I didn't think that I would ever sing and play again. But today while you were speaking I began to feel like I could start over. I can picture in my mind just what you are saying. I can do this. I know many musicians from all the churches in town. If you will pray for me, I will get to work.

Thirty minutes later, Joy was saying goodby. She put on her headset and started making calls while she drove. By 2 pm she had a half dozen musicians gathered in her living room. She explained to them what she and Caroline had discussed earlier. There was an excitement brewing among the group. Several of them had also felt that they should be more involved in the Truth meetings but they didn't know what to do other than pray. Now they all had a common purpose and after a few minutes of tuning their instruments they started to play and sing.

ఆఆఆఆఆఆఆఆఆఆఆఆఆఆఆఆ

Harriet stood in the front room that her grandmother used to call the parlor. It was a spacious room where her grandmother, and years later her mom, would entertain their friends. After both her mom and dad had died, she used it for a reading room and had lined the walls with her books. Off to the side sat her grandmother's piano. It was a baby grand that her mom had cherished. Harriet had learned to play when she was a small girl and kept up lessons even as an adult. After her attack, she had closed off the room. She hadn't felt like reading or playing her piano for a long time but today seemed different.

She had gone to church with her new friends and to her surprise she loved it. She even went back to the widow's house again on Tuesday. The Creatures of the Forest had not given up easily, as a matter of fact they had regrouped to try and figure out what was happening to Harriet. Something strange had happened to their strength. Every day they seemed weaker and weaker. Now she was sitting at the piano and was flipping through some music books that had been her grandmother's. After finding what she was looking for she started to play. The tune seemed vaguely familiar to the Creatures. By the time they remembered what it was, it was too late. Harriet started to sing. "I surrender all. I surrender all. All to Thee my precious savior. I surrender all."

The Creatures of the Forest were fading. Their greatest nightmare had come upon them. Harriet's spirit had been renewed. Feelings she had forgotten since she was a child came rushing upon her. Joy and Peace started flooding her heart all at once and she felt like she would burst. Laughter was bubbling from deep inside and she began to hold her sides while she laughed for the first time in a very, very long time. Jumping up from the piano bench, Harriet ran from the room, threw open the front door and jogged all the way down the street to the widow's house.

Caroline had just gotten off the phone with Joy when she heard her door bell ring. Wondering who it was she peeked out her window in time to see Harriet ring it again with impatience. She opened the door and started to ask what was wrong when she saw the pinched look that had been on Harriet's face was gone and she looked like a different person. In truth she was.

The whole story came out in a rush as Harriet tried to tell Caroline everything that had happened. Pulling the young woman by the arm and guiding her to the living room, Caroline told her to start over. Harriet left nothing out. She remembered every little detail, especially the part when she sang, "I surrender all."

After the excitement settled down a bit, Caroline asked Harriet if she would like some tea. She said yes and they moved to the kitchen. About the time the tea kettle was whistling, the phone rang. It was Joy.

"Oh Caroline. You should have heard us. The whole group of musicians came over and we played for a couple of hours. I can't wait to go to the prayer meeting tonight. I just know something good is about to happen. It was just perfect. Well, almost perfect. It would be even better if we had a keyboard player.. I have my sister's keyboard here at my house but I don't know anyone who can play it."

Caroline was no stranger to the workings of God. She had seen God work out his plans many times but they always caused her to pause and smile at his goodness. "Don't worry, Joy. I think God has that all worked out for you. I'll tell you about it tonight at the church." With that she hung up the phone.

Jesus is Truth
He is Creature Killing Truth

Chapter 15

His Word Is Truth

By 6:30 pm Pastor Steve's church was packed. Many people had heard about the fire that happened that morning in Pastor Mark's church. The whole church was buzzing with questions. At 7 pm, Steve went to the platform and took the microphone, "Attention everyone. Please can everyone take a seat? We really need to get started tonight with our prayer time but before we do I have asked Pastor Mark to give us all an update on what happened this morning."

Mark stood, off to the side of the platform, where he had been sitting. Steve handed him the cordless microphone. "Many of you know I live next door to my church. I couldn't sleep and was in my kitchen when I looked out the window and noticed smoke coming from the church. I called the fire department and the police. After they put the fire out they discovered that a man had died in that fire. This has all been very disturbing however we as your pastors in this community have committed to pray together. We believe that we are doing the right thing in having these Truth prayer meetings. We also believe that there are principalities and powers in the spirit realm that want to stop them. Sometimes in life we find that our lives have taken detours through dark and troubling times. We struggle to see the light and sometimes even doubt that it exists. It is in this forest of darkness that we find thoughts of depression, inferiority, shame, unforgiveness, or jealousy, to name a few. These are who we have been calling, the Creatures of the Forest. Jesus came to bring his light into that darkness! All the Creatures of the Forest run and hide in his light. He is glowing with an intensity that causes all the evil spirits of hell to run for cover. We are doing something significant and the workers of Darkness are unhappy. Please continue to come out every night for the rest of this week and the next. I believe we are going to see the Power of God in a mighty way." Finishing with those words, he handed the microphone back to Steve and sat down.

Steve then nodded to the Bishop who stood and took the microphone. "Brothers and Sisters," he boomed in his warm deep voice. "Let's all stand and pray. Heavenly Father, we have come once again to ask that you reveal the Truth to us. We need your power and strength. Your word is Truth and it sustains us in the midst of troubling times. Your son, Jesus Christ, is the Truth. It is this Truth that redeems us from the penalty of our sin. Through the power and infilling of your Holy Spirit we are set free by your Truth. Speak to us tonight. Calm our fears and fill us with courage. Thank you for what you have done and what you are about to do. We stand in agreement tonight, believing in your promises…"

The Bishop continued for another five minutes and then Grey took the microphone. As he was finishing, others were lining up beside him ready to pray. People began to go to their knees and prayers were being uttered between every bench and down every aisle. Warfare had begun.

Standing in the back of the church was Roger. He had been stunned to learn that his fire had not been more effective. He decided that he would come to the prayer meeting this night so he could better understand the layout of the church. However it seemed like a bad idea as the Creatures, who hung on him like shackles began to bite and tear at his thoughts. They were unhappy with the prayers and the unity that was evident in the church.

Once everyone started praying, he snuck down the back staircase to look around the basement. Down a long hallway, there were several rooms off to each side. At the end of the hall was a small kitchen and some restrooms. None of the doors were locked and all of the rooms looked to be some kind of classroom with tables and a chalkboard. There was a small room just off from the kitchen that had no window. It had shelves lining the walls and looked to be used only for storage.

This was the perfect place for a fire. He would get it right this time. As Roger walked back down the hallway, he entered one of the classrooms and carefully unlocked one of the windows. This is where he would get in.

About 1 am Roger returned, climbed through the basement window and walked back towards the storage room. Tonight was easier. He felt more sure of himself. Abandoning the bomb idea was right. Fires were much easier to deal with. The Creatures of the Forest had been pressing him all day to make sure of all his details. They didn't want another spoiled attack. After thinking his plan through several times, he was sure this church would not be standing by morning. In the storeroom, Roger found a large trash can. He filled it with rags and cardboard, set it next to the shelves containing cleaning products and threw in a lighted match. He lingered just long enough to make sure the fire was sufficient and hurried to the kitchen. The old gas cooking stove was easy to manipulate. He blew out the pilot light and turned on every burner. He could feel his adrenaline surging as he ran back down the hallway, scurried through the window he had come in and sprinted to his truck he had left two blocks away.

છ છ છ છ છ છ છ છ છ છ છ છ છ છ છ છ

The explosion happened at about 1:45 am. It lit up the sky with a flash and the sound echoed off every building. People jumped out of their beds wondering what had happened and some could see the fire and smoke from as far as 10 miles away. It was a bit cloudy that night and some mistook the smoke for rain. But it didn't take long for everyone to realize that something bad had happened. Flames began to shoot upwards and more explosions echoed as the fires engulfed the shed out back where leftover paint had been stored.

It took several fire departments working side by side to get the fire under control. It was a good thing that the church was set back from the area housing development or the fire could have taken several houses as well as the church. Nevertheless, had the wind shifted that night it could have been a lot worse. It seemed like everyone up and down the local streets had come running from their homes in slippers and robes to see what was happening. By morning there were still a few firemen and local police but the flames were gone and all that was left were glowing coals where once had stood a lovely old church.

About ten minutes after the initial explosion, Steve and Caroline heard the phone ring and they knew before anyone said a thing that the sound that had woken them up had come from their church building. "Mom, stay here," Steve said as he flew out the door with his keys and a thermos of coffee in his hand.

Caroline had made the coffee while Steve had run up the stairs to dress. Now she stood on her front porch watching her son go. "Oh Lord be with him she whispered." A tear ran down her cheek as she closed the door and sighed.

ೞೞೞೞೞೞೞೞೞೞೞೞೞೞೞ

Steve was driving a bit faster that he should have, and grabbing his cell phone he started calling first Mark then Grey. They both agreed to call the remaining pastors from the area and promised to meet him at the fire. A half hour later, twenty pastors from every denomination were gathered around Steve. Standing ramrod straight but with tears in his eyes he embraced each one. No one said a word. At that point there wasn't much to say.

CREATURES OF THE FOREST

Replace Your Thoughts By: Praying and Speaking Truth

Chapter 16

A Public Declaration

Mark called Joy and asked her to go over to the widow's house. When she got there, she didn't even wait for Caroline to answer the door but opened it herself, ran straight towards her, and folded her in her arms. The older woman had been sitting by the front window in her favorite recliner but she hadn't been resting. She had been silent, praying in her heart, her eyes dripping with tears. Not even realizing Joy was there until she was caught in the sisterly embrace, she shuddered and then the tears came in a flood. The Creatures of the Forest were reveling in Caroline's grief but when Joy showed up they were quick to leave in fear that they would be seriously wounded. These two women had the potential to break their power, if not totally destroy them. They wouldn't take any chances.

An hour later, both women were holding steaming cups of tea and nibbling on toast. They had been sitting that way for several minutes when Caroline spoke up. "Joy, I'm so glad you came over. I was so worried when Steve left and then my imagination got the best of me. I played so many scenarios over in my mind and I just couldn't understand what had happened. Did we have a gas leak in the church? Did we leave the coffee pot on? How did the fire start? Was it my fault? My body still feels like it's shaking but my spirit has settled some."

"I know," Joy responded. "I was pretty shook up myself. However I know that God is with us. Last night at the prayer meeting, I sat on the edge of my seat knowing that something big was about to happen. Then, afterward, when you told me about Harriet, it confirmed what I already knew, that God was at work. So I spoke to Harriet just before we all left your church. She is all set to meet me this afternoon to look over music. Caroline, I honestly don't remember the last time I saw anyone so excited about finding Jesus."

಄಄಄಄಄಄಄಄಄಄಄಄಄಄಄಄

Harriet marveled at the change she felt deep inside. If anyone had mentioned, even a few short days ago, that she would experience such a change, she would have scoffed at them. Now today, she was once again sitting at the piano, only today she was going over all of the new music Joy had given her. She wasn't very adept at figuring out the music by ear but thankfully, Joy had given her the sheet music that went with the program for that night. Flipping through the pages she tried each song while the peace that surrounded her protected her from the Creatures of the Forest. Many times she shook her head wondering why this peace had alluded her for so long, and why it was hers now. Then she remembered that it was the moment when she surrendered everything to Jesus that he had given her this amazing peace.

She'd played the first three songs over several times when the phone rang. It was Joy. "Harriet, there has been a fire at the church we were at last night. The whole church has burnt down and Caroline wanted to know if you would be available to play for a special prayer meeting that she is calling for this afternoon. We are going to meet at the Community Center at 2 pm."

಄಄಄಄಄಄಄಄಄಄಄಄಄಄಄಄

There was a bee hive of conversations going on at the Center. Harriet was warming up her fingers, getting used to the electric keyboard and Joy was tuning her guitar. People were gathered in little groups, some praying together and others chatting about the fire. There were so many unanswered questions. What started the fire? How could this be? Why would God allow something like this to happen when we have been having such unity? And, who is behind all of this anyways?

Pastor Steve was there and called the meeting to order. "Hello everyone," he said with an even stronger voice than he thought he possessed. "My mom and I have asked you all here today to stand in prayer with us and our church family. As many of you know, we have been under some kind of attack. These attacks are not random but thought out and planned. Ever since we started praying, we have been the target of vandalism, lies, and now arson. Obviously we are doing something right, or the spirits of Darkness, or the Creatures of the Forest as we have been calling them, wouldn't be so intent on discouraging us from our times of prayer. In unity, we have been praying, for the Truth to be revealed. Jesus is the Truth and we will not stop seeking him. He is our helper and our healer. He is our strength and our light through difficult times. Without him we are nothing. He is the Way, the Truth, and the Life."

"Today," Steve continued. "I am making a public declaration that we will not cease to pray. As a matter of fact, we are going to step up our prayers and add to them, times of worship. God has gathered together a musical group that, I believe, will help us as we pray. Music calmed the evil spirit attacking King Saul's mind and he will use it to calm our shaken spirits. Not only that, but we will see God move more and more. I believe we are about to see God's Holy Spirit, in a new way that will impact the generations to come. Please don't give in to the Creatures of the Forest. Fear has been whispering to us all and we have to silence him. He is a most dangerous creature and he has many friends who can do us great damage as well. Our unity is being attacked and also the very nature of Truth itself. So please come out to prayer with an even greater dedication. Encourage your friends to come. We have an opportunity that many only dream of having. Let's not lose it." Steve finished and then sat down.

At almost the same moment, the newly formed musical group started to play. Scripture put to music, old tried and true choruses, and new, more contemporary music blended together, capturing the moment in worship in ways that most in the room had never experienced before. Steve recognized Joy and some of the other musicians but he didn't remember ever seeing the petite young woman playing the keyboard. Not only was he captivated by the skill by which her fingers glided over the keys but her sparkling green eyes caused him to catch his breath every time he looked at her.

After an hour of worship and another in prayer Steve closed the meeting and announced to the group that there would be a meeting that night in the Bishop's church, just as planned.

ຽຽຽຽຽຽຽຽຽຽຽຽຽຽຽ

Roger was sitting on the front step of his shop, smoking a cigarette. Lucy hated it when he smoked and so he did most of his smoking on that step. Today, instead of enjoying the few minutes he had to himself, he began to mull over, in his mind, the events of the past few days. The Fearlings were causing him a great deal of grief. They kept telling him that he was going to be found out. They were stirring up feelings that caused Roger to loathe himself. "Look what you have done. You have killed a man and set fires in two churches. Someone will have seen you. It's only a matter of time before someone calls the police. They will find you….find you….find you." Anger was adding his two cents worth as well, "Let them catch me. I've done nothing wrong except trying to right the wrongs that have been done to me. I don't care if the whole world finds out that I am the one who has been doing these things. I'll take them all down with me. I'll expose the filthy preacher who stole my wife. He won't get away with it. I'll take down all of his friends too." All reason had left Roger and he thought he would grow mad from the voices in his head. Finally after several hours of inner turmoil he decided that tonight he would do nothing. He needed the sleep.

Jesus is Truth
He is Creature Killing Truth

Chapter 17

A Few Nights Of Peace

It was the second night in a row that the prayer meetings were held in the Bishop's church. Most of the churches in town were too small to host the meetings. It was an amazing night as the music group played for over an hour and then a Holy hush came over the whole congregation. Some people seemed stuck in their seats while others fell to the floor on their knees. Everyone began to pray at almost the same time and soon a cacophony of prayers could be heard from all corners of the room. Even in the kitchen, where some of the ladies were preparing for the snack and fellowship after the prayers, there were people on the floor praying. Suddenly a solitary tune was heard coming from the electric keyboard. "I surrender all. I surrender all. All to Thee my blessed Savior, I surrender all. Before the first few lines were finished the whole room began to sing as one. "I surrender all!"

Steve looked up as Harriet's fingers effortlessly glided over the keys. Who was this person? Steve had taken great pains to talk to as many people as he could, every night. Yet somehow he had missed Harriet. He would have to search her out as soon as the meeting was over.

Fearlings had been stationed at every window. Fear was a powerful weapon and the Creatures of the Forest often sent them out ahead of the rest. If Fear could get a foothold into anyone's spirit, then other Creatures had an opportunity to find willing hearts as well. If the people in the room had been able to see into the realms of the dark spirit world, they may have been affected by the sheer number of Fearlings. However each one's eyes seemed to be fixed on the wall behind the musical group. On both sides of the stage, there were TV screens displaying the words to the songs being played by the newly formed band. Hanging on the back wall of the platform was a cross made from rough cut timber. While everyone sang, their eyes gazed from the cross to the words. No one noticed the Creatures gazing in the windows. As each song was played, the message of the cross became stronger and stronger and the Fearlings became weaker and weaker. Watching themselves shrinking in size right before their very own eyes, they turned with a puff and scurried away.

Roger had fully intended to attend the meeting. He had scheduled all of his repair work at his garage to be done in the morning so he could prepare for another fire. He was struggling with his emotions as he made phone calls to various auto suppliers looking for the parts he needed. He had just finished calling the third place, looking for a specific part for an antique car. The extra money he would get from these repairs seemed to make it worth the aggravation however he was not in a good mood and he slammed the phone down on his desk. As he did, his fist came crashing down with it, shattering his coffee cup. The cup was one he had had for years. Several times it had fallen from his desk to the floor, never breaking, however this time, it shattered in several pieces, leaving three large shards imbedded in Roger's hand. Blood was everywhere and it appeared that the gashes needed stitches.

Cursing under his breath, Roger hastily wrapped his hand in a paper towel, closed up his shop, and drove to the ER. The waiting room was full and Roger was passed over several times as more serious cases came in. Five hours later he was finally on his way home. He had had several stitches and his hand was bandaged up looking like a baseball catchers mitt. There would be no fire tonight or the next few nights either.

ःःःःःःःःःःःःःःःः

Steve was standing in the back of the church, three nights later. The musical group had been playing every night and practicing every afternoon. They were flowing together as if they had done this for years. Steve loved to hear them play but he was more captivated by the petite woman playing the keyboard. He had fully intended to introduce himself to her a few nights ago but there were so many people who were hovering around him, offering their sympathy and prayers, that he couldn't get away. She always seemed to slip away by the time he was free.

The next morning over coffee and omelets he asked Caroline about her. "Mom, who is it that plays the piano? I don't ever remember seeing her before the musical group was formed. Is she someone who comes to your prayer group on Tuesdays?"

"Oh, you mean Harriet? Yes she comes on Tuesdays. She is new to our group. However she lives just down the street. You know that house at the end, where no one ever seems to come or go from? Well that is her house. The Lord put it on my heart to visit her. At first she was reluctant but then somehow in God's special way, he touched her. She has been really hurt somehow. I don't know what happened but she is growing in her relationship with the Lord by leaps and bounds now. When she first came she was a bundle of nerves. But now she is a brand new person. I have been so happy to watch her. Isn't she a fabulous keyboard player?"

As a matter of fact Harriet had been growing in her relationship with the Lord at a rapid rate. Once the power of the Creatures of the Forest had been broken, her mind had been released from their grip. She stopped listening to their voices and her spirit was free. While others may take years to grow to the level she had come to, she had grown closer and closer each day. She was reading her Bible and it was healing her mind. She had no idea that it was God's word that would release her mind but she knew she felt better every time she read.

At first what she read was confusing to her. The Creatures of the Forest had commissioned Confusion to sit by her. She had been comfortable with Confusion. He had been her personal companion for a long time. He could speak to her and she would think that what he said were her own thoughts. He would whisper, "I don't understand. I don't understand. How can God's word help me if I don't understand?" And Harriet believed him.

She was almost ready to quit reading when a verse popped out at her. It was as if she were wearing three dimensional glasses. The words were life. She had been reading in 1 Peter. Unbeknownst to her, the Holy Spirit had been gently drawing her to those passages. When she got to chapter two, verse ten jumped out at her. She had a new translation of the Bible which made the reading a little easier. "Once you were nobody but now you belong to God." (This is my own translation. DLD). That was so true. It was just like Widow Foster had told her, the Truth had set her free. Now she belonged to God. At that moment her whole life changed. After all these years she finally knew who she was. She was God's daughter. He loved her and she belonged to him.

Now, when she sat at the keyboard to play it was as if a new person played. She sang while she played and her whole being was immersed in the presence of God. The Creatures of the Forest were losing their grip on her more and more each day. Soon they were in a panic. "What to do? What to do?" They cried. However Harriet wasn't listening to them. The Truth had truly set her free.

That night the prayer meeting was gathering at Grey's church and the music group was there early to practice. Steve was there too but not to practice. He was hoping to get a moment with Harriet.
After an hour and a half, the music group was ready to go home, get a bite to eat, and return back for the evening service. Steve had stepped into Grey's office to talk over some of the program for the evening and almost missed Harriet as she walked out of the door. Sprinting after her, he reached her as she took out the keys to her car. "Hi, I'm Steve. I believe you know my mom, Caroline."

"Oh yes. Yes I do. I recognized you from the portrait she has of you on her fireplace mantle."

Steve hadn't thought past introducing himself and there was an uncomfortable gap in time as each of them tried to think of something to say. He broke the silence and asked, "Would you like to go have a sandwich and a cup of coffee? We have enough time to do that. That is if you would like to."

Suddenly Fear, who had been trailing behind them, jabbed Harriet in her side and the pain shot into her heart causing her to feel ice cold. She hadn't had any personal interaction with a man since her abduction. Now all the peace she had been experiencing for the last several days seemed gone and Panic had a grip on her throat. With wild eyes she shook her head, jumped into her car and drove away. The Creatures of the Forest were back.

Replace Your Thoughts By: Praying and Speaking Truth

Chapter 18

Making The Truth Our Own

Steve was shocked by Harriet's reaction. Why was she afraid of him? What had he done? She didn't seem like a fearful person and yet when he spoke to her, her whole demeanor had suddenly changed. What had he done to cause such fear? "Mom," *he* said as he walked into the house. "Can we talk?"

Caroline told Steve about how scared Harriet had been the first time she saw her. She suggested that he approach her slowly if he wanted to get to know her. "I don't know anything about Harriet's past but something has happened to her. I had forgotten that I knew her parents. They lived in the same house down the street where Harriet lives now. She had gone away to school and came back sometime after her parents had died. Her grandmother used to come to our church and I remember her bringing Harriet with her sometimes."

Down the street, Harriet was in a full blown panic. Creatures were laughing and mocking her. "Just who do you think you are? You have no right to talk to someone like Steve. You will never be able to have a relationship with a man. You are damaged goods. You're broken and there is no hope for you. What makes you think you will ever be free. That freedom you felt was only temporary. You can't escape. You can't escape. You can't...." With that Harriet broke out in a cold sweat and collapsed on her bed.

Suddenly like warm water flowing over her body she remembered a song her grandmother used to sing over her. "Jesus loves me this I know..." Mumbling under her breath she sang until she fell into a deep sleep. Then in a dream she saw herself being carried on the wings of angels. She could hear Jesus talking to her. "Peace, my peace I give to you. Not as the world gives but my peace I give to you. Don't be afraid my little one." As she floated over dark clouds, she could see the darkness in them. Fear and hopelessness were in the darkness of the clouds. She could hear the Creatures of that darkness crying. She began to understand that she was no longer subject to their wishes and words. She was being carried up up up over the darkness until their voices faded away. She wasn't afraid any more. She felt the weight of the Creatures fall from her and she could see a crystalline river in the distance.

As she floated on the angelic wings they drew closer and closer to that water and Jesus began to speak to her again. "Harriet, I have redeemed you, you are mine. When you walk through difficult times I will be there. I will never leave you. I will always be there for you. Don't be afraid of tomorrow. I have a plan for your life. It is a good plan. Do not fear your tomorrows for you are mine. You are loved and you will be loved. Look forward and not backward. Because this is a new day." As she drew closer and closer to the river she realized it wasn't a river at all but a man. She knew instantly that the man was Jesus. It seemed like the water was flowing over him yet through him. He was overwhelmed by the water but not carried away. He was smiling as the angels dropped her in his arms and the river flowed over and over her while the words, "I am the river of Life. He who drinks from me will never thirst again," echoed through her spirit.

When she awoke, she wasn't sure what time it was or how long she had been asleep. She remembered every part of the dream, if it was a dream. Did she dream or had she been carried away in some spiritual experience? Not really understanding all that had just happened to her, she was struck with the reality that what she had experienced had been real. Very real.

She looked at the clock and realized that she had just enough time to change her clothes, drink a quick smoothie and drive to the evening meeting. Hopefully she would arrive in time to warm up her fingers on the keyboard before they had to start.

છ3છ3છ3છ3છ3છ3છ3છ3છ3છ3છ3છ3છ3છ3છ3

Pastor Grey and Steve were standing at the back door welcoming people as they entered the stately old church. When Harriet arrived she breezed past them giving them both a smile as she hurried up to the platform. She didn't have time to chit chat at the door but her smile was enough to bewilder Steve.

Roger was back. He had been frustrated because of his injury. His hand had swollen and turned red. He obviously had an infection in the wound. He had to make an appointment with his doctor to get some antibiotics. Just as he was getting back in his truck, Lucy drove up. She must have had an appointment with the doctor too. Their eyes met just for a second when Lucy turned away. He never saw the pain and sorrow of his rejection in her eyes. He just saw her turn and walk away. Assuming she could care less about him, he slammed his truck door and sped off. Rejection was sitting beside him as he drove. "She despises you. She hates you. She loves another man." It didn't take much to put Roger in a sour mood.

He was hoping Lucy would see him come to the church. He had some choice words he wanted to say to her. She would regret rejecting him. He would make her pay for the pain he felt. Unfortunately, she was already seated when he arrived and he had no desire to walk to the front of the church while the service was about to begin.

Roger started snooping as soon as the music started and people stood to sing. After the fire at Steve's church he was feeling pretty bold. This church would be easier since it was down a dark street close to the city park. He would be able to come and go during the night and not risk being seen.

The Creatures had been hounding him all day. Hatred was consuming him. Failure was constantly reminding Roger that none of the pastors had died and neither had anyone else except Ben. "You've failed, you've failed. You haven't set a fire in three days. You've failed, you've failed." The pain he had endured in his hand, was just enough to push him over the edge. He was no longer able to control himself. Most of the time his hands shook from the anticipation of violence. His head ached from too much drinking and not enough sleep, yet his adrenaline was kicking and his heart was pounding.

In the large meeting room Grey was addressing the gathering. "Brothers and sisters," he said. "Three nights ago, after our prayer meeting at Pastor Steve's church building, a fire broke out and consumed the entire structure. By the time the fire department had arrived there was little they could do. I'm sure most of you are aware of the situation that also happened at Pastor Mark's church. This dear old building has also suffered damage when the beautiful stained glass window was broken. I'm sure there are some of you here who are starting to become afraid. In the last few months Steve's mom, Widow Foster, has been holding some effective ladies meetings in her home. They are Truth Meetings. They started out being a little gathering for some of her neighbors but they have grown to be much more. I have asked her to share some of what God has been doing with her little group. I believe she has some insight that we should be using in our Truth prayer meetings." With that said, Grey handed the microphone to Caroline and then sat down.

The widow stood and began to tell everyone what she had felt the Lord had been speaking to her. Then she shared some of the scriptures she had been using to make the Truth real in her life. "For example, dear friends. Right now I am telling myself the truth. You see I could be consumed with fear. It was my church building that burnt. Yes, it belonged to our whole church body but it was my husband who had the dream and the vision to build it. He had faith for every detail. He labored until late many nights to finish projects so that our building would be a blessing to our congregation. I remember when the rafters for the roof went up and when the tile in the restrooms were laid. I wrapped my husband's blistered hands after he worked for hours hanging the dry wall. So in a sense, that building felt like an extension of me. So when it burned… well, the Creatures of the Forest attacked me with fear. I thought I was immune to the Creature's attack. I have been studying the Word of God almost my whole life. I knew that God was my helper and my guide but in the last few weeks I have been challenged to make Jesus my Truth. He is the Truth. He is the reason we have hope for our tomorrows. So this is what I have been doing."

At this point Caroline started a PowerPoint presentation. On it were two columns. The left column listed negative feelings or situations. On the right were Truth scriptures that related to the corresponding feelings. "This is not intended to be vain repetition," Caroline continued. "But concentrated ownership. We have to use every way available to us, in order to make the Truth our own. We speak Truth. We pray Truth. We memorize Truth. We share Truth with each other. We listen to music or sing along with music that gives a truthful message. We remind ourselves with the truth by putting stickers and posting notes all over our house. We take ownership of Truth and then it begins to work in our lives. We own Truth. It is ours!"

"The Bible says that Abraham believed what was not, as though it were. He was believing the Truth. Just because our situation doesn't look like truth, doesn't mean that Jesus isn't working all things for our good. Abraham believed the truth before he saw it. He believed in Truth and God called him righteous for believing. Too often we see our lives and we don't like what we see. We believe in what we see because our nature says that seeing is believing. We see with our natural eyes, things we do not like, and we wish that these things didn't exist. We need to change our mentality. We are people of faith. Believing God for what we can't see isn't a lie. No! It is the truth manifested in our lives. We believe therefore we respond to what we believe. If you believe that Satan is a liar and that there is no truth in him then we must conclude that God is Truth.

I want to challenge you to make these scriptures your own and if you don't find what you need then study your Bible. Ask your pastor for help. Call on your friends, help each other. The Word of God is Truth. Jesus is the Word and Jesus is Truth. And the Truth works. I have seen Him work in my life and I have seen Him work in the lives that gather with me every week. Not only that but He is working right now, I could rail against God or complain because of the fire that destroyed our church building. But I choose to believe that no weapon formed against me shall prosper. I choose to believe that if God is for me then there is no power greater that can stand against me. I choose to believe that God is working all things out for my good. Philippians 4:8 says, Finally, brethren, whatsoever things are true, whatsoever things *are* honest, whatsoever things *are* just, whatsoever things *are* pure, whatsoever things *are* lovely, whatsoever things *are* of good report; if *there be* any virtue, and if *there be* any praise, think on these things. Let us be mindful of what the Lord is saying to us today. We need to change our thoughts. If we do this, it will change how we speak and how we pray. It will change us all in powerful ways. I am excited to see what God is about to do. Obviously something good must be happening for the devil to be so angry that he is attacking us with such violence."

Caroline turned and handed the microphone back to Grey and he stood to address the crowd. "From now on, we are going to change the way we pray. Every request for prayer will be coupled with a scripture that speaks truth. Some of us are afraid tonight. So, tonight we will pray and as we do so, we will believe that Truth will prevail. No weapon formed against us will prosper. God will have the upper hand and whoever is terrorizing us, will be found and he will be stopped. We also stand with each and everyone of you. The situations you face in your lives are no less serious. So we stand with you and believe that God will reveal his truth to you. Please if you need help finding corresponding scriptures ask one of us pastors to help. We would be glad to do so. Some of us have been calling the lies attacking us, Creatures of the Forest. They want to steal your joy and make you give up. Like Mrs. Foster said, we are people of faith and I for one, choose to live like one. Tonight I declare war on the Creatures of the Forest." With those words came a cheer that reverberated throughout the building.

All around the room people began to pray. Some were standing and others were kneeling. Hands were folded and heads bowed while other hands were lifted high. There was weeping and tears mingled with shouts of passion as people from every denomination began to wage war with the Creatures of Darkness.

Roger was taken off guard when he heard the shouting. He wondered what it could mean but decided that the noise made a good cover and he continued making his plans. Leaving a few windows open, he snuck out the back door and walked through the park to get an idea of the path he would take later that night.

CREATURES OF THE FOREST

ෆෆෆෆෆෆෆෆෆෆෆෆෆෆෆෆ

Harriet had been sitting at the piano perfectly still for a very long time. Her mind had been working overtime since she had started playing with the music group. It seemed like the fears that plagued her were getting smaller and smaller while songs and melodies began to well up within her. Songs she remembered her grandmother singing, and songs she had never known before yet seemed very familiar. She had talked to Joy about it and she told her they were a special gift from the Holy Spirit. She had never really known the Holy Spirit before but he was fast becoming her friend. It seemed like he grew larger in her spirit while the Creatures of the Forest grew smaller every day. It was an odd way to put it but that is how she felt. It was happening again as she sat on the bench. She closed her eyes and just let her fingers brush the keys not knowing that it was the very Spirit of God that was moving her hands. Then out of her mouth came a sigh and with it the words, "Holy Spirit, I'm yours."

Soon the whole room was whispering, shouting, and singing those words. It seemed like the world stood still. People up and down the rows took in a breath like it was their very first. Burdens began to fall from the backs of those in the room. No, they didn't see their heavy burdens fall but they felt them as they did. One by one they fell and one by one the people, throughout the room, began to weep with joy. Many had never felt anything like this before but no one doubted that they had been touched by God.

Jesus is Truth
He is Creature Killing Truth

Chapter 19

The Power of Testimonies

Never knowing how close his church was to being burnt down, Bishop Wallace invited everyone back to his church for Saturday night and every night for the next week. His was the only building large enough to accommodate the amount of people gathering every night. If the crowds continued to get bigger, they might need to move to the ball field or school auditorium sooner than they originally thought. Everyone would be going to their own churches the next morning and this Saturday night proved to be a great celebration. Most of the people in the city had never experienced a revival before. They didn't know what to expect from the Truth meetings and were surprised at how simple and powerful the Word of God was when applied as Truth in their lives. The last couple of nights had only built with expectation upon each other.

That night there were twice as many people out. The pastors all agreed that they needed time to allow people to give their testimonies about what God had been doing in their lives. There were so many that they could only have a few share however, Janey Fisher, Steve's secretary, took it upon herself to interview as many people as she could and then she typed out their stories, printed them, and handed them out to people as they arrived. The whole room was buzzing. There had been no more attacks and everyone had decided that the worst was over. Everyone still wondered who was behind the fires and vandalism. Just that morning the papers were reporting on the man found dead at the first fire in Mark's church. His identity had done nothing to help answer the questions. No one seemed to be able to connect him to any of the churches or the rumors going around town. As a matter of fact Ben was quite unknown. He had no family except for a brother who had moved to Alaska when he was young. He was making plans to arrive sometime in the next few days to settle Ben's estate.

Steve smiled when he looked at Harriet playing the keyboard. They had gone out for coffee a few times now and it looked like they just might become more than just friends. Every time he looked at her she seemed more beautiful. "This just might be love," he mumbled as he watched her play. It didn't hurt any that his mom loved her too.

C3CICICICICICICICICICICICI3

Sunday morning, every church in town was full. People were buzzing about, retelling their testimonies of what God had done for them. Several people had received a significant healing. There had been the old man, who lived on Pine street. He had been deaf for twenty years. Friday night, while everyone was praying, he stood up shouting that he could hear. There was a little girl, about seven years old. She had never walked. Her growth was stunted and her back was twisted in a strange way. In the middle of one of the worship songs, her back started making strange cracking sounds. She seemed almost lifted from her wheelchair and started running. Her face beaming, she was still running three days later. Several people who had been plagued with depression had physically felt a cloud lift off from them. Couples were falling in love all over again and arguments had been forgotten.

One man stood up, with tears running down his face. He told of all the times his father had abused him and then he confessed that he had been abusing his own wife and son in the same way his father had. Then he fell to his knees, first in front of his wife and then to his son, begging them to forgive him. The testimonials were so many and so wonderful that most of the pastors never had a moment to preach. Those that did, used their time to challenge their congregation to start telling themselves the Truth.

CICICICICICICICICICICICICI

That night, Roger stopped off at the corner bar on his way home. It had become a habit. He would stop in, have a few drinks, eat or not eat depending on the menu, and then go home. This night he drank a little more than usual. He was celebrating his plans and future victory. Feeling proud of himself he continued to order drinks. The next thing he knew, he was sleeping in his truck, parked on the same dead end street he had found himself on before. Only this time, he had lost two whole days. He was befuddled and nauseous. How did he get there? How did he lose so much time?

The Creatures had also been celebrating. They were so proud of their control of Roger that they encouraged him to keep drinking. They clouded his mind and broke down any remaining thoughts of decency. They lied to him over and over. "No, you are not a drunk. You are not out of control. Just to prove how much control you have, order one more drink." Some Creatures were irritated with Roger's drinking but he told them to leave him alone. People in the bar could hear him arguing with himself not knowing there was a spiritual battle going on. He stayed as long as could and staggered out of the bar. He made it back to his home only to continue drinking what he had in the house. Sometime, in the darkest hours of the night, he got into his truck, thinking that he was going to the church. How he got to the dead end road, he never knew.

He looked at the sign on the edge of the road.

DEAD END

Dead. He felt dead. "Is this what death feels like?" He asked himself. He couldn't take his eyes off the sign. Dead. Dead. Dead. Dead.

Confusion had been twisting Roger's mind to the point that he didn't know Confusion's ideas from his own. Bombs, fire, murder. Bombs, fire, murder. What to do? What to do? He thought he should concentrate his efforts on how he could kill Steve. Should he go back to the bomb idea? Should he kidnap Steve, secure him in one of the churches and burn him along with the building? Never in his wildest dreams had he thought he would become a murderer but now that was all he could think about. Murder and Hatred consumed him. Roger decided he would forget about burning the church buildings. The fires had not stopped the churches from praying, as a matter of fact, they seemed to ignite a spiritual fire that he couldn't understand. Besides he didn't feel the gratification he expected when he burnt Steve's church to the ground. It wasn't enough to burn the churches. Pastor Steve should be dead. Dead. Dead. Dead. There would be no more fires. Once Steve Foster was dead, he would be satisfied.

 C3CXC3C3C3CXC3C3CXC3C3CXC3C3CXC3

Roger was happy to hear that the next few meetings would still be in the Bishop's church. There was an outside door right off to the right of the platform. It was be an easy entrance, once the meeting got started. He didn't go inside. He didn't need to. He had been there for a wedding a few months back and remembered the side door. The groomsmen had entered the front of the church from there. He would do the same thing when the time was right. Tonight he just sat in his truck thinking. After an hour, he headed towards Ben's house.

Roger didn't own any guns but Ben had. There were several in his house. There was a rifle cabinet in the basement and a pistol case in his bedroom. Ben had showed them to Roger a while back. The rifles had been Ben's dad's. The pistols however, were Ben's pride and joy. He has been collecting them since he was old enough to own one.

Just as Roger was about to pull into the driveway, he saw a rental car sitting in the driveway. Lights were on in Ben's house. The curtains were all open and someone was walking around the place talking on his cell phone. Roger didn't know what to do, so he parked his truck down the street and waited for the stranger to leave. After about ten minutes several police cars pulled into Ben's driveway right behind the rental car.

Sam, Ben's brother, had arrived that afternoon to settle his brother's estate. He had stopped at his hotel, taken a quick shower and grabbed something to eat before heading over to the house. When he arrived he quickly saw that Ben had been involved in something bad. Something very bad. He called the police and they promised to come right over. In the mean time, he looked around the place, careful not to touch anything in case the police needed to take fingerprints. There were empty beer cans and bomb making materials sitting around the kitchen table. The whole place reeked of rotting food and marijuana.. Sam knew about the rifles and were among the first things he had looked for. They were all locked up in their glass case. He was glad they had not been involved in whatever else Ben had been up to. He didn't know about the pistols since he had left home when Ben was only sixteen and that was before Ben started his collection..

Roger could only hope that the police didn't find the pistols. They were hidden in Ben's bedroom. Roger had only seen them once. Ben told him that he kept them in a special case in his bedroom but he never said where in his bedroom. It took a couple of hours for the police to finish their investigation of Ben's house and Roger was getting anxious. He didn't know how much longer he could stay parked down the street without drawing attention. Finally about 8:30 pm they left. Roger waited another twenty minutes just to make sure no one had forgotten anything and returned. He casually walked up the street and checking to see if anyone saw him, he snuck around to the back of the house. He knew where Ben kept a hidden key. Letting himself in the back door, he walked through the house and up the stairs to Ben's bedroom in the dark. With a pen light between his front teeth, Roger tore open every drawer and closet in the bedroom. He flipped over the mattress and fumbled through the nightstand. Ben had never been a good housekeeper but his room now looked like a tornado had landed in the room. Thinking the police had found the pistols Roger cursed under his breath and started to leave the room when he saw the box sitting on a shelf next to the television. It never occurred to him that they would be in plain sight. He opened the box, took out one of the pistols and grabbed a new box of ammunition that also sat on the same shelf. The next day, the police would see that their crime scene tape forbidding anyone to enter had been broken and the bedroom in shambles.

Replace Your Thoughts By: Praying and Speaking Truth

Chapter 20

The Truth Prevails

Thursday night, proved to be the biggest attendance yet. The Creatures were freaking out. They hated the Truth and they especially hated testimonies. Every time someone testified about Jesus healing them or someone being set free from the Creature's influence, they cringed. The testimonies built faith in those who heard and the Creatures were shrinking. Everyday their power was diminished and the people who listened to their lies became fewer and fewer. Creatures were sending SOS messages to their cousins around the country but so far the prayers of the people, had given power to angelic forces that were growing everyday. Almost no evil reinforcements had been able to enter Brooks Glen. Even those who passed through the barriers were handicapped from their fight to enter the city. By the time they reached the rest of the Creatures of the Forest, they were barely able to withstand the prayers on their own let alone help the ones who had been there from the beginning.

The Bishop was busy talking to the music group and most of the other pastors were busy welcoming everyone as they came in. Steve, however, was busy talking to Harriet. It seemed he couldn't get enough of her. Her green eyes captivated him and he wanted to spend every minute with her. Even though their relationship was still too new to talk about marriage, both Harriet and Steven had hoped it would end that way. Nether of them could imagine life without the other. Caroline had been encouraging them by inviting Harriet over for dinner and late night chats about the meetings over tea and cookies.

When the meeting was called to order, the musicians all took their place. Joy had taught them a new song that afternoon and they opened the meeting with it. The song was a modern twist on the old hymn Just As I Am. The Bishop felt that this night would be a night to remember. He believed that the Lord was directing him to ask those who were there to rededicate their lives to the Lord. They had seen so many miracles and so much healing that he was concerned that the people might be coming only to see what God was doing. He felt challenged in his own heart that he take some time to turn his focus back to the Lord Jesus.

By the time the song was finished, everyone stood to their feet, lifted their hands towards heaven. With tears streaming down many of the faces they all were whispering, "I come, I come." Then as if a great choir master were standing in the front directing the whole of the room, the drums began to pound, the guitars responded to their beat and the whole room began to resound with worship. The Holy Spirit began to touch one after another as they worshiped. That night, the work of the Holy Spirit was beyond anything, any of them had ever experienced before. Soon there were as many people on their knees bowing before the magnificence of God's Spirit as there were standing to attention before their King, The King of Kings. And he was doing a marvelous work in all of their lives. It was a night they would never forget.

ඃඎඃඎඃඎඃඎඃඎඃඎඃඎඃඎඃඎ

Roger had walked into the back entryway just as the music was starting and the Creatures that had attached themselves to him were clawing at his mind. Fear was trembling, "What to do oh, what to do?" In one moment he would tell Roger to walk right up to the front and shoot Steve and then the next he was screaming for his life fearful of what might happen to him should they walk into the presence of God. Confusion was actually have a grand old time making fun of Fear and scrambling Roger's mind. Hatred seemed the most protected. He had gained an entrance into Roger's heart and was puffing himself up with each step Roger took. With a murderous look Roger looked around the church. Was Lucy there, he wondered? He wanted her to be there when he shot Steve. She would be horrified of course but that was what she deserved.

Harriet was playing the keyboard and the Holy Spirit took control of her fingers. She began to play a heavenly melody that matched the feeling of the room. Steve was standing next to her, worshiping with tears falling from his eyes.

Suddenly there was a sound from a woman sitting in the front row of the room. She screamed the word gun and pointed at Roger as he walked up to Steven, coming from the side door of the platform. Pointing the pistol at Steve, he hissed, "I'm gonna kill you preacher. I'm gonna kill you right in front of all these people. You deserve what you get for stealing my wife."

Lucy was sitting in the back on the right side of the church and heard Roger's voice as soon as he spoke. "Roger, is that you? Roger what are you doing? Where did you get that gun? Put it away Roger. Stop!"

He just glared at her with glassy eyes. "Shut up woman. I'm gonna kill your preacher then I'm gonna kill you!" With that he waved his pistol around the room so everyone would know he meant business.

Harriet started to whimper. Fear had snuggled up to her on the bench that she sat on. He had once been welcomed by her. He was hoping she would welcome him back. He missed her.

Steve looked straight at Roger. "Roger, it's me. You know me. Why do you want to kill me? I have done nothing to your wife. This is all a great misunderstanding. Roger, listen to me."

Roger was twitching and sweat was pouring down his face. His hands were shaking not from fear but rage. Hatred had transformed himself into a monster and he loved the way Roger responded to him. "Shut up! Shut up! All of you shut up!" He cursed and swung the pistol towards the congregation for emphasis. Somewhere in the back someone started chanting, something like cheerleaders at a football game, only this was not a chant to encourage the local football team. No, it was the Name of Jesus. "Jesus, Jesus, Jesus." People clapped their hands and stomped their feet. The drummer started to pound the rhythm with his drums and Harriet swept the bench with her hand as if to brush away the spirit who was trying to attach himself to her. She started playing with the drums. "Jesus! Jesus! Jesus!" The whole room began to shake from the power of that name.

Steve looked at Roger and commanded, "Roger, drop that gun. In the Name of the Lord God almighty, Jesus Christ, drop that gun."

With mighty swords, the name of Jesus engraved on the blade in their hands, angelic warriors stood ready for battle. Not a word was said as they stood at attention waiting for the order to attack. Steve and those on the platform stood frozen in place. Looking at the gun that was pointed directly at them they didn't even blink an eye.

Suddenly the gun fell from Roger's hands as if it were burning hot. When it fell, it went off shooting Roger in the leg. The bullet struck an artery and blood began to spurt out as he slumped to the ground. His mind was being squeezed by the angry Creatures because he failed to fulfill his mission. Hatred was beating him like His dad used to do. He was screaming in anguish.

Lucy ran to the front and disregarding the danger of the situation, ran to Roger, knelt to the floor and wrapped her arms around him. "Why Roger?" She asked as she realized that Roger had been the one responsible for all of the attacks. "Why? Why did you do these things?"

Roger, ignoring the pain, resisted Lucy and grabbed the gun that had fallen close to where he lay. "Shut up woman," he growled. Then with Hatred coursing through his veins, he pulled himself up. "Why? He shouted. "Why? I'll tell you why. That man. That man you call your preacher, took you from me. When you asked for a divorce, I realized it was because you had fallen in love with him."

"No, Roger. No! I have only ever loved you. I only asked for a divorce from you because you didn't love me anymore. I don't love Pastor Steve. I never have. I have only ever loved you."

Someone in the church had called 911 as soon as Roger had showed up waving the gun. There was already an unmarked police car at the church, with many more on their way. When detectives had arrived at Ben's house that day, they saw that it had been broken into and the bedroom ransacked. After interviewing people up and down the street they had learned that someone driving that old pickup truck had been there many times including the night before. Roger had become a person of interest in Ben's death. So, as soon as they discovered who the owner of the truck was, they began to have an unmarked car follow him.

The State trooper who had been following Roger, had also followed him into the church. "Drop it!" He said, in a voice that commanded obedience. By now the other troopers and the local sheriff had arrived and were taking positions around the church.

The Creatures were screaming at Roger. His head felt like it would split in two. "Shoot! Shoot! Roger! Shoot! The preacher deserves to die!" At the same time the words Lucy had spoken to him began to resonate deep within his heart. "I love you Roger. I have always loved you."

Roger's eyes were wild and he pointed the gun, first at Steve and then at Lucy. "No I saw you! I saw you go into that church during the week to be with him. I saw you. No!" he screamed. He opened his mouth to say more but it was as if he were cut off from his own thoughts.

No earthly words were spoken as the whole congregation stood still. Then as Roger started to pull the trigger, another voice was heard. It was the Bishop. "Not by might. Not by power says the Lord! Put the gun down sir. In the Name of Jesus, I command you! In the Name of Truth, in the Name of the Lord God Almighty, PUT THE GUN DOWN!"

Once again the gun fell to the floor with Roger following. The Creatures were scrambling in fear. "The Name!" They cried. "He used the Name! He used the Name! He used the Name! Oh what to do? What to do?" Quickly each Creature scrambled to leave as fast as he could. Disappearing in puffs of smoke they left Roger whimpering on the floor.

Lucy knelt down beside Roger realizing that he wouldn't live long. The wound in his leg had steadily been pumping out blood and he was growing paler by the minute. The pastors in the front gathered around Lucy and Roger. Harriet began to play some soft music, while Joy flipped through her music. When she came upon the right song she whispered. "Ok everyone, let's start with, 'I Surrender All!" Soon the whole congregation began to softly sing.

Now that Roger had been released by the Creatures of the Forest, he started to cry, "Oh Lucy , forgive me. I was so consumed by guilt that I couldn't even look at you. Oh Lucy, I haven't been faithful to you. When I saw you go to see that Pastor, I felt justified. I thought you had been unfaithful to me too. Oh Lucy I'm so sorry. Can you ever forgive me? Do you think God will ever forgive me? I've done terrible things."

"If you believe, Roger. Yes I forgive you and God will too, if you believe. Believe in Jesus, Roger. Believe in the Truth. He will set you free."

"I believe." Roger whispered as he drew his last breath and died.

ෲෲෲෲෲෲෲෲෲෲෲෲෲෲෲ

There were plenty of stories that went around about that night. Some say that they saw angels. Others saw a cloud fill the room. One man was sure he saw a giant hand reach down and grab Roger by the arm. Few agreed on all the details but they all agreed that God had worked a miracle that night.

Off in the distance, the Creatures of the Forest had gathered. "Defeated! Defeated!" the Creatures of the Forest cried. "Oh what to do now....what to do?" A little creature in the back squeaked, "Crawford, we can go to Crawford. There's no prayer meetings there." Off they flew in broken whips of smoke.

ෲෲෲෲෲෲෲෲෲෲෲෲෲෲෲ

Early the next morning, in the local coffee shop, Steve and Mark sipped at their coffee reflecting on everything that had been happening for the last few weeks.

In the middle of their conversation, Steve looked up at Mark with an excited expression on his face. "I have a great idea Mark!"

"I'm all ears," Mark replied.

"Lets go over to Crawford tomorrow. I have a friend there. He could call up a few of the pastors and set up an impromptu meeting. I want to tell them about all the things that have been going on here. They need to know about the miracles and healings taking place. They need to start their own Truth prayer meetings. What do you say, Mark? Are you with me?"

"Absolutely!" came the reply.

Proverbs 4:18-26
But the path of the righteous is like the bright morning light, growing brighter and brighter until full day. The way of the wicked is like gloomy darkness; they do not know what causes them to stumble. My child, pay attention to my words; listen attentively to my sayings. Do not let them depart from your sight, guard them within your heart; for they are life to those who find them and healing to one's entire body. Guard your heart with all vigilance, for from it are the sources of life. Remove perverse speech from your mouth; keep devious talk far from your lips. Let your eyes look directly in front of you and let your gaze look straight before you. Make the path for your feet level, so that all your ways may be established. Do not turn to the right or to the left; turn yourself away from evil
NET

Ephesians 4:17-24
This I say therefore, and testify in the Lord, that ye henceforth walk not as other Gentiles walk, in the vanity of their mind, Having the understanding darkened, being alienated from the life of God through the ignorance that is in them, because of the blindness of their heart: Who being past feeling have given themselves over unto lasciviousness, to work all uncleanness with greediness. But ye have not so learned Christ; If so be that ye have heard him, and have been taught by him, **as the truth is in Jesus**: That ye put off concerning the former conversation the old man, which is corrupt according to the deceitful lusts; And be renewed in the spirit of your

mind; And that ye put on the new man, which after God is created in righteousness and true holiness.
KJV

Epilogue

Sometimes in life we find that our lives have taken detours through dark and troubling times. We struggle to see the light and sometimes even doubt that it exists. It is in this forest of darkness that we find thoughts of depression, inferiority, shame, unforgiveness, or jealousy, to name a few. These are the Creatures of the Forest.

Jesus came to bring his light into this darkness! All the Creatures of the Forest run and hide in his light. He is glowing with an intensity that causes all the evil spirits of hell to run for cover.

Young and old, rich and poor, we all battle the Creatures of the Forest. Everyone of us fight the thoughts of darkness. These thoughts are designed to steal our hope, our joy, and our peace. They want to consume us with despair and hopelessness and in the process trap us into the aimless life of defeat. They deceive and confuse us, making us believe the truth for a lie and a lie for the truth.

However we are not without the answer. The answer is Jesus. He is our hope. He is our peace. He is our joy. He is the way. He is the truth. He is our life. You see truth isn't a concept he is a person. The reason why Truth sets us free is because Jesus sets us free. When we replace the lies of darkness with the truth of Jesus everything changes. The reason many people never experience freedom is because they either don't know Jesus or they haven't taken ownership of the truth that is in Him. It isn't enough to hear about the truth. It isn't enough to read about the truth. You have to own the truth. You have to replace the lies of darkness by believing in the truth more than you believe in the lie. So many people never realize true freedom because the voices in their heart and mind have deceived them into believing that there is no hope. They resign themselves to a life of defeat instead of a life of victory.

It only takes one person to set evil in motion. Once he gains a foothold, he grants authority to other evil powers and a chain reaction occurs. Likewise, it only takes one person to hear from God and to lead others in the good fight of faith. However one person alone can not carry out what it takes to combat the works of Darkness. It takes the body of Christ coming together with a common goal, laying aside our differences and realizing that there is nothing more important than the household of God. Then as we depend on the authority of the cross and it's power through the work of the Holy Spirit, we take our rightful place in the Kingdom of God. It is then that the works of Darkness are shattered. In the face of this united front none of the Creatures of Darkness can stand.

The Word of God is true and He works in our lives. We have the responsibility to make every one of our thoughts obedient to Christ.

He is the answer, the Way, the Truth, and the Life.

In Him we live and have our being.

In Him is Life and the Light of that Life.

The Truth

1. We have all sinned.
2. We all need a Savior.
3. Jesus died for us while we were still sinners.
4. God loved us so much that he gave us his only Son, Jesus.
5. Salvation is a free gift from our Heavenly Father. All you have to do is accept his gift.
6. We have not been left alone to deal with thoughts of darkness.
7. We have been given God's Holy Spirit to comfort and to guide us.
8. You can make it.
9. You can live a victorious life.
10. You can have mental health.
11. You can find freedom.
12. It's not too late.
13. You are not too far gone.
14. There is Hope and his name is Jesus.
15. Healing is for us today.
16. Believe the Truth and He will set you free!
17. You must make the Truth your own.
18. You must do spiritual battle every day.
19. God has given us the ability to fight
20. You can win.

Our Weapons

2 Corinthians 10:3-5
For though we walk in the flesh, we do not war after the flesh: (For the **weapons of our warfare** are not carnal, but mighty through God to the pulling down of strong holds;) Casting down imaginations, and every high thing that exalteth itself against the knowledge of God, and bringing into captivity every thought to the obedience of Christ

Ephesians 6:10-18
Finally, my brethren, be strong in the Lord, and in the power of his might. Put on the whole armour of God, that ye may be able to stand against the wiles of the devil. **For we wrestle not against flesh and blood, but against principalities, against powers, against the rulers of the darkness of this world, against spiritual wickedness in high** *places*. Wherefore take unto you the whole armour of God, that ye may be able to withstand in the evil day, and having done all, to stand. Stand therefore, having your loins girt about with truth, and having on the breastplate of righteousness; And your feet shod with the preparation of the gospel of peace; Above all, taking the shield of faith, wherewith ye shall be able to quench all the fiery darts of the wicked. And take the helmet of salvation, and the sword of the Spirit, which is the word of God: Praying always with all prayer and supplication in the Spirit, and watching thereunto with all perseverance and supplication for all saints

Scriptures Fit For Battle

THE FOLLOWING SCRIPTURES ARE A SPRINGBOARD FROM WHICH YOU CAN START TO DO BATTLE AGAINST THE CREATURES OF THE FOREST. READ THESE VERSES IN DIFFERENT VERSIONS OF THE BIBLE, ADD OTHER VERSES, AND MAKE THESE TRUTHS YOUR OWN.

Anger

<u>You say</u>: "I can't control my anger."
<u>God says</u>:" By the power of my Holy Spirit, you can."

Psalms 37:8-9
Cease from anger, and forsake wrath: fret not thyself in any wise to do evil. For evildoers shall be cut off: but those that wait upon the LORD, they shall inherit the earth.

Proverbs 16:22
Understanding *is* a wellspring of life unto him that hath it: but the instruction of fools *is* folly.

James 1:19-20
Wherefore, my beloved brethren, let every man be swift to hear, slow to speak, slow to wrath: For the wrath of man worketh not the righteousness of God.

Proverbs 15:1
A soft answer turneth away wrath: but grievous words stir up anger.

Proverbs 14:29
He that is slow to wrath *is* of great understanding: but *he that is* hasty of spirit exalteth folly.

Anxiety

You say: I am so afraid and anxious. I am paralyzed with fear.
God says: Fear not for I am with you. I will never leave you or abandon you. You are mine.

Proverbs 3:5-6
Trust in the LORD with all thine heart; and lean not unto thine own understanding. In all thy ways acknowledge him, and he shall direct thy paths.

Philippians 4:6-7
Be careful for nothing; but in every thing by prayer and supplication with thanksgiving let your requests be made known unto God. And the peace of God, which passeth all understanding, shall keep your hearts and minds through Christ Jesus.

Luke 12:22-34
Therefore I say unto you, Take no thought for your life, what ye shall eat; neither for the body, what ye shall put on. The life is more than meat, and the body *is more* than raiment. Consider the ravens: for they neither sow nor reap; which neither have storehouse nor barn; and God feedeth them: how much more are ye better than the fowls? And which of you with taking thought can add to his stature one cubit? If ye then be not able to do that thing which is least, why take ye thought for the rest? Consider the lilies how they grow: they toil not, they spin not; and yet I say unto you, that Solomon in all his glory was not arrayed like one of these. If then God so clothe the grass, which is to day in the field, and to morrow is cast into the oven; how much more *will he clothe* you, O ye of little faith? And seek not ye what ye shall eat, or what ye shall drink, neither be ye of doubtful mind. For all these things do the nations of the world seek after: and your Father knoweth that ye have need of these things. But rather seek ye the kingdom of God; and all these things shall be added unto you.
 Fear not, little flock; for it is your Father's good pleasure to give you the kingdom. Sell that ye have, and give alms; provide yourselves bags which wax not old, a treasure in the heavens that faileth not, where no

thief approacheth, neither moth corrupteth. For where your treasure is, there will your heart be also.

Psalms 55:22-23
Cast thy burden upon the LORD, and he shall sustain thee: he shall never suffer the righteous to be moved. But thou, O God, shalt bring them down into the pit of destruction: bloody and deceitful men shall not live out half their days; but I will trust in thee.

1 Peter 5:7
Casting all your care upon him; for he careth for you.

ೞೞೞೞೞೞೞೞೞೞೞೞೞೞೞೞ

Bad Thoughts
You say: I can't control my thoughts.
God says: With my help you can.

Philippians 4:8
Finally, brethren, whatsoever things are true, whatsoever things *are* honest, whatsoever things *are* just, whatsoever things *are* pure, whatsoever things *are* lovely, whatsoever things *are* of good report; if *there be* any virtue, and if *there be* any praise, think on these things

Ephesians 3:17-19
That Christ may dwell in your hearts by faith; that ye, being rooted and grounded in love, May be able to comprehend with all saints what *is* the breadth, and length, and depth, and height; And to know the love of Christ, which passeth knowledge, that ye might be filled with all the fulness of God.

2 Corinthians 10:5
Casting down imaginations, and every high thing that exalteth itself against the knowledge of God, and bringing into captivity every thought to the obedience of Christ;

Proverbs 4:23
Keep thy heart with all diligence; for out of it *are* the issues of life.

Betrayal

You say: I can't trust any one. I have been so betrayed.
God says: I understand. I have been betrayed too. Let me carry this burden for you.

Hebrews 4:15-16
For we have not an high priest which cannot be touched with the feeling of our infirmities; but was in all points tempted like as [we are, yet] without sin. Let us therefore come boldly unto the throne of grace, that we may obtain mercy, and find grace to help in time of need.

Psalms 41:2
The LORD will preserve him, and keep him alive; *and* he shall be blessed upon the earth: and thou wilt not deliver him unto the will of his enemies.

Psalm 55:22
Cast thy burden upon the LORD, and he shall sustain thee: he shall never suffer the righteous to be moved.

Romans 8:28
And we know that all things work together for good to them that love God, to them who are the called according to *his* purpose.

ഗഗഗഗഗഗഗഗഗഗഗഗഗഗ

Condemnation

You say: I feel so guilty. I am ashamed.
God says: Come to me and lay your guilt at my feet. You need not be ashamed.

John 3:16-17
For God so loved the world, that he gave his only begotten Son, that whosoever believeth in him should not perish, but have everlasting life. For God sent not his Son into the world to condemn the world; but that the world through him might be saved.

Romans 8:1
There is therefore now no condemnation to them which are in Christ Jesus, who walk not after the flesh, but after the Spirit.

Isaiah 50:9
Behold, the Lord GOD will help me; who *is* he *that* shall condemn me?

Psalms 34:22
The LORD redeemeth the soul of his servants: and none of them that trust in him shall be desolate.

Zephaniah 3:15
The LORD hath taken away thy judgments, he hath cast out thine enemy: the king of Israel, *even* the LORD, *is* in the midst of thee: thou shalt not see evil any more.

രുരുരുരുരുരുരുരുരുരുരുരുരുരു

Confusion

You say: I don't know what to do. I am so confused.
God says: Hold my hand and let me lead you in the way you need to go.

Daniel 2:20-22
Blessed be the name of God for ever and ever: for wisdom and might are his: And he changeth the times and the seasons: he removeth kings, and setteth up kings: he giveth wisdom unto the wise, and knowledge to them that know understanding: He revealeth the deep and secret things: he knoweth what *is* in the darkness, and the light dwelleth with him.

1 Corinthians 15:33
Be not deceived: evil communications corrupt good manners

Proverbs 3:5-6
Trust in the LORD with all thine heart; and lean not unto thine own understanding. In all thy ways acknowledge him, and he shall direct thy paths.

Isaiah 41:10
Fear thou not; for I *am* with thee: be not dismayed; for I *am* thy God: I will strengthen thee; yea, I will help thee; yea, I will uphold thee with the right hand of my righteousness.

అఅఅఅఅఅఅఅఅఅఅఅఅ

Debts

You say: I have so much debt. I will never be able to get out from under them.
God says: I will provide all your needs. Give me control of your finances and see what I can do for you.

Deuteronomy 28:12
The LORD shall open unto thee his good treasure, the heaven to give the rain unto thy land in his season, and to bless all the work of thine hand: and thou shalt lend unto many nations, and thou shalt not borrow.

Psalms 84:11
For the LORD God *is* a sun and shield: the LORD will give grace and glory: no good *thing* will he withhold from them that walk uprightly.

Philippians 4:19
But my God shall supply all your need according to his riches in glory by Christ Jesus.

2 Corinthians 9:6-11
But this *I say*, He which soweth sparingly shall reap also sparingly; and he which soweth bountifully shall reap also bountifully. Every man according as he purposeth in his heart, *so let him give*; not grudgingly, or of necessity: for God loveth a cheerful giver. And God *is* able to make all grace abound toward you; that ye, always having all sufficiency in all *things*, may abound to every good work: (As it is written, He hath dispersed abroad; he hath given to the poor: his righteousness remaineth for ever. Now he that ministereth seed to the sower both minister bread for *your* food, and multiply your seed sown, and increase the fruits of your righteousness;) Being enriched in every

thing to all bountifulness, which causeth through us thanksgiving to God.

೧೩೧೩೧೩೧೩೧೩೧೩೧೩೧೩೧೩೧೩೧೩೧೩೧೩

Distrust

You say: I have been so hurt. I am afraid to trust again.
God says: I know your pain. Trust in me and I will protect you.

Hebrews 2:13
And again, I will put my trust in him.

Psalms 26:1
Judge me, O LORD; for I have walked in mine integrity: I have trusted also in the LORD; *therefore* I shall not slide.

Nahum 1:7
The LORD *is* good, a strong hold in the day of trouble; and he knoweth them that trust in him.

Psalm 9:10
And they that know thy name will put their trust in thee: for thou, LORD, hast not forsaken them that seek thee.

೧೩೧೩೧೩೧೩೧೩೧೩೧೩೧೩೧೩೧೩೧೩೧೩೧೩

Fear

You say: I am so afraid. I have no peace.
God says: I am here with you. I will protect you and hold you in my arms. Do not fear.

Psalms 55:22
Cast thy burden upon the LORD, and he shall sustain thee: he shall never suffer the righteous to be moved.

Psalms 56:3
What time I am afraid, I will trust in thee.

John 14:27
Peace I leave with you, my peace I give unto you: not as the world giveth, give I unto you. Let not your heart be troubled, neither let it be afraid.

Isaiah 35:4
Say to them *that are* of a fearful heart, Be strong, fear not: behold, your God will come *with* vengeance, *even* God *with* a recompence; he will come and save you.

Joshua 1:9
Have not I commanded thee? Be strong and of a good courage; be not afraid, neither be thou dismayed: for the LORD thy God *is* with thee whithersoever thou goest.

Matthew 6:34
Take therefore no thought for the morrow: for the morrow shall take thought for the things of itself. Sufficient unto the day *is* the evil thereof.

Psalms 25:20
O keep my soul, and deliver me: let me not be ashamed; for I put my trust in thee.

You say: "I'm afraid"
God says: I have not given you a spirit of fear.

II Timothy 1:7
For God hath not given us a spirit of fear, but of power, and of love, and of a sound mind.

You say: "I don't have enough faith"
God says: I've given everyone a measure of faith

Romans 12:3
For by the grace given me I say to every one of you: Do not think of yourself more highly than you ought, but rather think of yourself with sober judgment, in accordance with the measure of faith God has given you. NIV

Isaiah 41:10
Fear thou not; for I [am] with thee: be not dismayed; for I [am] thy God: I will strengthen thee; yea, I will help thee; yea, I will uphold thee with the right hand of my righteousness.

1 John 4:18
There is no fear in love; but perfect love casteth out fear: because fear hath torment. He that feareth is not made perfect in love.

Psalms 23:1-6
(A Psalm of David.) The LORD [is] my shepherd; I shall not want. He maketh me to lie down in green pastures: he leadeth me beside still waters. He restoreth my soul: he leadeth me in the paths of righteousness for his name sake. Yea though I walk through the valley of the shadow of death, I will fear no evil:for thou art with me; thy rod and thy staff they comfort me. Thou preparest a table before me in the presence of mine enemies: Thou anointest my head with oil; my cup runneth over. Surely goodness and mercy shall follow me all the days of my life: and I will dwell in the house of the Lord forever.

Psalms 34:4
I sought the LORD, and he heard me, and delivered me from all my fears.

Proverbs 29:25
The fear of man bringeth a snare: but whoso putteth his trust in the LORD shall be safe.

Philippians 4:6
Be careful for nothing; but in every thing by prayer and supplication with thanksgiving let your requests be made known unto God.

Psalms 56:3-4
What time I am afraid, I will trust in thee.

Romans 8:15
For ye have not received the spirit of bondage again to fear; but ye have received the Spirit of adoption, whereby we cry, Abba, Father.

Romans 8:38-39
For I am persuaded, that neither death, nor life, nor angels, nor principalities, nor powers, nor things present, nor things to come.

Isaiah 43:1-3
But now thus saith the LORD that created thee, O Jacob, and he that formed thee, O Israel, Fear not: for I have redeemed thee, I have called [thee] by thy name; thou [art] mine.

Proverbs 19:23
The fear of the LORD tendeth to life: and he that hath it shall abide satisfied; he shall not be visited with evil.

ଔଔଔଔଔଔଔଔଔଔଔଔଔଔ

Forgiveness
<u>You say</u>: "I can't forgive myself"
<u>God says</u>: I forgive you.

I John 1:9
If we confess our sins, he is faithful and just to forgive us our sins, and to cleanse us from all unrighteousness.

Romans 8:1-2
There is therefore now no condemnation to them which are in Christ Jesus, who walk not after the flesh, but after the Spirit. For the law of the Spirit of life in Christ Jesus hath made me free from the law of sin and death.

Ephesians 4:32
And be ye kind one to another, tenderhearted, forgiving one another, even as God for Christ's sake hath forgiven you.

Matthew 6:15
But if ye forgive not men their trespasses, neither will your Father forgive your trespasses.

1 John 1:9
If we confess our sins, he is faithful and just to forgive us [our] sins, and to cleanse us from all unrighteousness.

Matthew 18:21-22
Then came Peter to him, and said, Lord, how oft shall my brother sin against me, and I forgive him? till seven times? Jesus saith unto him, I say not unto thee, Until seven times: but, Until seventy times seven.

Matthew 6:14-15
For if ye forgive men their trespasses, your heavenly Father will also forgive you:

James 5:16
Confess [your] faults one to another, and pray one for another, that ye may be healed. The effectual fervent prayer of a righteous man availeth much.

Luke 6:27
But I say unto you which hear, Love your enemies, do good to them which hate you,

Luke 6:37
Judge not, and ye shall not be judged: condemn not, and ye shall not be condemned: forgive, and ye shall be forgiven:

Colossians 3:13
Forbearing one another, and forgiving one another, if any man have a quarrel against any: even as Christ forgave you, so also [do] ye.

Psalms 103:10-12
He hath not dealt with us after our sins; nor rewarded us according to our iniquities. For as the Heaven is high above the earth, so great is his mercy toward them that fear him. As far as the east is from the west, so far hath he removed our transgressions from us.

1 Corinthians 10:13
There hath no temptation taken you but such as is common to man: but God [is] faithful, who will not suffer you to be tempted above that ye are able; but will with the temptation also make a way to escape, that ye may be able to bear it.

ଔଔଔଔଔଔଔଔଔଔଔଔଔଔଔ

Grief

<u>**You say**</u>: My heart is so sad.
<u>**God says**</u>: Trust me. The time of weeping will soon be over and you will smile again.

Psalms 30:5
Weeping may endure for a night, but joy *cometh* in the morning.

Psalm 25:2
O my God, I trust in thee: let me not be ashamed, let not mine enemies triumph over me.

Psalm 62:8
Trust in him at all times; *ye* people, pour out your heart before him: God *is* a refuge for us.

Nahum 1:7
The LORD *is* good, a strong hold in the day of trouble; and he knoweth them that trust in him.

ෲෲෲෲෲෲෲෲෲෲෲෲෲෲෲෲ

Hatred

<u>You say</u>: I am consumed with hatred.
<u>God says</u>: I can help you. Be consumed with me.

Luke 6:35-36
But love ye your enemies, and do good, and lend, hoping for nothing again; and your reward shall be great, and ye shall be the children of the Highest: for he is kind unto the unthankful and *to* the evil. Be ye therefore merciful, as your Father also is merciful.

Proverbs 10:12
Hatred stirreth up strifes: but love covereth all sins.

James 1:19-20
Wherefore, my beloved brethren, let every man be swift to hear, slow to speak, slow to wrath: For the wrath of man worketh not the righteousness of God.

Psalms 4:4
Stand in awe, and sin not: commune with your own heart upon your bed, and be still.

ෲෲෲෲෲෲෲෲෲෲෲෲෲෲෲෲ

Hurts and Pain

You say: My heart is so heavy. I feel so much pain.
God says: I know your pain and I care for you. Trust me.

Revelation 21:4
And God shall wipe away all tears from their eyes; and there shall be no more death, neither sorrow, nor crying, neither shall there be any more pain: for the former things are passed away.

Psalm 25:18
Look upon mine affliction and my pain; and forgive all my sins.

Psalms 32:7
Thou *art* my hiding place; thou shalt preserve me from trouble; thou shalt compass me about with songs of deliverance.

Psalm 119:114
Thou *art* my hiding place and my shield: I hope in thy word.

ഗ3ഗ3ഗ3ഗ3ഗ3ഗ3ഗ3ഗ3ഗ3ഗ3ഗ3ഗ3ഗ3ഗ3

I'm tired

You say: I can't make it even one more day. I am so weary.
God says: I am your strength.

Romans 8:9
But ye are not in the flesh, but in the Spirit, if so be that the Spirit of God dwell in you.

Galatians 6:9
And let us not be weary in well doing: for in due season we shall reap, if we faint not.

Matthew 11:28-30
Come unto me, all *ye* that labour and are heavy laden, and I will give you rest. Take my yoke upon you, and learn of me; for I am meek and lowly in heart: and ye shall find rest unto your souls. For my yoke *is* easy, and my burden is light.

Psalms 62:1-2
Truly my soul waiteth upon God: from him *cometh* my salvation. He only *is* my rock and my salvation; *he is* my defence; I shall not be greatly moved.

Psalms 46:1
God *is* our refuge and strength, a very present help in trouble.

ѠѠѠѠѠѠѠѠѠѠѠѠѠѠѠѠ

I hate myself
<u>**You say**: I am ugly. I am worthless.</u>
<u>**God says**: I love you. I created you and you are</u>
<u>beautiful to me. I have a purpose and future for you.</u>

1 Corinthians 6:19-20
What? know ye not that your body is the temple of the Holy Ghost *which is* in you, which ye have of God, and ye are not your own? For ye are bought with a price: therefore glorify God in your body, and in your spirit, which are God's.

1 Corinthians 3:16
Know ye not that ye are the temple of God, and *that* the Spirit of God dwelleth in you?

Psalms 139:14
I will praise thee; for I am fearfully *and* wonderfully made: marvellous *are* thy works; and *that* my soul knoweth right well.

Luke 12:22-31
And he said unto his disciples, Therefore I say unto you, Take no thought for your life, what ye shall eat; neither for the body, what ye shall put on. The life is more than meat, and the body *is more* than raiment. Consider the ravens: for they neither sow nor reap; which neither have storehouse nor barn; and God feedeth them: how much more are ye better than the fowls? And which of you with taking thought can add to his stature one cubit? If ye then be not able to do that thing which is least, why take ye thought for the rest? Consider the lilies how they grow: they toil not, they spin not; and yet I say unto you, that Solomon in all his glory was not arrayed like one of these. If then God so clothe the grass, which is to day in the field, and to morrow is cast into the oven; how much more *will he clothe* you, O ye of little faith? And seek not ye what ye shall eat, or what ye shall drink, neither be ye of doubtful mind. For all these things do the nations of the world seek after: and your Father knoweth that ye have need of these things. But rather seek ye the kingdom of God; and all these things shall be added unto you.

1 Peter 2:9-10
But ye *are* a chosen generation, a royal priesthood, an holy nation, a peculiar people; that ye should shew forth the praises of him who hath called you out of darkness into his marvellous light: Which in time past *were* not a people, but *are* now the people of God: which had not obtained mercy, but now have obtained mercy.

C3C3C3C3C3C3C3C3C3C3C3C3C3C3

Impossible Situations
You say: "It's impossible"
God says: All things are possible.

Luke 18:27
Jesus replied, "What is impossible with men is possible with God." NIV

જીજીજીજીજીજીજીજીજીજીજીજીજીજીજી

Injustice

You say: People have treated me wrong.
God says: Trust me, I will make it right.

2 Corinthians 12:9
My grace is sufficient for thee: for my strength is made perfect in weakness.

Hebrews 2:14-15
Forasmuch then as the children are partakers of flesh and blood, he also himself likewise took part of the same; that through death he might destroy him that had the power of death, that is, the devil; And deliver them who through fear of death were all their lifetime subject to bondage.

Colossians 3:15-17
And let the peace of God rule in your hearts, to the which also ye are called in one body; and be ye thankful. Let the word of Christ dwell in you richly in all wisdom; teaching and admonishing one another in psalms and hymns and spiritual songs, singing with grace in your hearts to the Lord. And whatsoever ye do in word or deed, *do* all in the name of the Lord Jesus, giving thanks to God and the Father by him.

Romans 12:21
Be not overcome of evil, but overcome evil with good.

જીજીજીજીજીજીજીજીજીજીજીજીજીજીજી

Loneliness

You say: I feel so much loneliness inside.
God says: Let me into your heart. I love you and I will be there for you. I have never left you.

Psalms 68:6
God setteth the solitary in families:

Romans 8:31-39
What shall we then say to these things? If God *be* for us, who *can be* against us? He that spared not his own Son, but delivered him up for us all, how shall he not with him also freely give us all things? Who shall lay any thing to the charge of God's elect? *It is* God that justifieth. Who *is* he that condemneth? *It is* Christ that died, yea rather, that is risen again, who is even at the right hand of God, who also maketh intercession for us. Who shall separate us from the love of Christ? *shall* tribulation, or distress, or persecution, or famine, or nakedness, or peril, or sword? As it is written, For thy sake we are killed all the day long; we are accounted as sheep for the slaughter. Nay, in all these things we are more than conquerors through him that loved us. For I am persuaded, that neither death, nor life, nor angels, nor principalities, nor powers, nor things present, nor things to come, Nor height, nor depth, nor any other creature, shall be able to separate us from the love of God, which is in Christ Jesus our Lord.

Psalms 27:10
When my father and my mother forsake me, then the LORD will take me up.

Isaiah 54:5
For thy Maker *is* thine husband; the LORD of hosts *is* his name; and thy Redeemer the Holy One of Israel; The God of the whole earth shall he be called.

Need Peace

<u>**You say**</u>: My life is in so much turmoil. I can't even sleep.
<u>**God says**</u>: I am your peace. I will never leave you alone.

Luke 10:19
Behold, I give unto you power to tread on serpents and scorpions, and over all the power of the enemy: and nothing shall by any means hurt you.

1 Peter 3:12
For the eyes of the Lord *are* over the righteous, and his ears *are open* unto their prayers: but the face of the Lord *is* against them that do evil.

Colossians 3:15
And let the peace of God rule in your hearts, to the which also ye are called in one body; and be ye thankful.

Isaiah 54:4
Fear not; for thou shalt not be ashamed: neither be thou confounded; for thou shalt not be put to shame: for thou shalt forget the shame of thy youth, and shalt not remember the reproach of thy widowhood any more.

C3C3C3C3C3C3C3C3C3C3C3C3C3C3C3

Need Understanding

<u>**You say**</u>: I don't know what to do. I don't understand what God wants me to do.
<u>**God says**</u>: I will give you wisdom and direct your steps.

Psalms 32:8
I will instruct thee and teach thee in the way which thou shalt go: I will guide thee with mine eye.

Psalms 27:11
Teach me thy way, O LORD, and lead me in a plain path,

1 Corinthians 2:9-10
But as it is written, Eye hath not seen, nor ear heard, neither have entered into the heart of man, the things which God hath prepared for them that love him. But God hath revealed *them* unto us by his Spirit: for the Spirit searcheth all things, yea, the deep things of God.

John 16:12-15
I have yet many things to say unto you, but ye cannot bear them now. Howbeit when he, the Spirit of truth, is come, he will guide you into all truth: for he shall not speak of himself; but whatsoever he shall hear, *that* shall he speak: and he will shew you things to come.He shall glorify me: for he shall receive of mine, and shall shew *it* unto you. All things that the Father hath are mine: therefore said I, that he shall take of mine, and shall shew *it* unto you.

James 1:5-6
If any of you lack wisdom, let him ask of God, that giveth to all *men* liberally, and upbraideth not; and it shall be given him. But let him ask in faith, nothing wavering. For he that wavereth is like a wave of the sea driven with the wind and tossed.

Colossians 3:16-17
Let the word of Christ dwell in you richly in all wisdom; teaching and admonishing one another in psalms and hymns and spiritual songs, singing with grace in your hearts to the Lord. And whatsoever ye do in word or deed, *do* all in the name of the Lord Jesus, giving thanks to God and the Father by him.

Poverty

You say: I have so many bills. I never have enough money.
God says: I will provide for every need you have.

Matthew 7:7-8
Ask, and it shall be given you; seek, and ye shall find; knock, and it shall be opened unto you: For every one that asketh receiveth; and he that seeketh findeth; and to him that knocketh it shall be opened.

Matthew 21:22
And all things, whatsoever ye shall ask in prayer, believing, ye shall receive.

John 15:7
If ye abide in me, and my words abide in you, ye shall ask what ye will, and it shall be done unto you.

Philippians 4:19
But my God shall supply all your need according to his riches in glory by Christ Jesus.

1 John 3:22
And whatsoever we ask, we receive of him, because we keep his commandments, and do those things that are pleasing in his sight.

ෆෆෆෆෆෆෆෆෆෆෆෆෆෆෆ

Rejection

You say: Nobody loves me. I am all alone.
God says: I love you with an everlasting love. You are mine.

Psalms 27:10
When my father and my mother forsake me, then the LORD will take me up.

1 John 3:1
Behold, what manner of love the Father hath bestowed upon us, that we should be called the sons of God:

Romans 8:38-39
For I am persuaded, that neither death, nor life, nor angels, nor principalities, nor powers, nor things present, nor things to come, Nor height, nor depth, nor any other creature, shall be able to separate us from the love of God, which is in Christ Jesus our Lord.

Ephesians 3:17-19
That Christ may dwell in your hearts by faith; that ye, being rooted and grounded in love, May be able to comprehend with all saints what *is* the breadth, and length, and depth, and height; And to know the love of Christ, which passeth knowledge, that ye might be filled with all the fulness of God.

ଔଔଔଔଔଔଔଔଔଔଔଔଔଔଔଔ

Ridicule
<u>**You say**: I have been rejected and humiliated.</u>
<u>**God says**: I have never rejected you and I will help you</u>
<u>through all of your troubles.</u>

Psalms 34:17-19
The righteous cry, and the LORD heareth, and delivereth them out of all their troubles. The LORD *is* nigh unto them that are of a broken heart; and saveth such as be of a contrite spirit. Many *are* the afflictions of the righteous: but the LORD delivereth him out of them all.

Romans 8:1
There is therefore now no condemnation to them which are in Christ Jesus, who walk not after the flesh, but after the Spirit.

1 Peter 4:14
If ye be reproached for the name of Christ, happy *are ye*; for the spirit of glory and of God resteth upon you

2 Corinthians 12:9
And he said unto me, My grace is sufficient for thee: for my strength is made perfect in weakness. Most gladly therefore will I rather glory in my infirmities, that the power of Christ may rest upon me.

രുരുരുരുരുരുരുരുരുരുരുരുരുരു

Shame and Guilt

<u>**You say**: I feel so ashamed. I have done so many bad things.</u>
<u>**God says**: If you give me your life I will take your shame and make you into a new person.</u>

Psalms 25:20-21
O keep my soul, and deliver me: let me not be ashamed; for I put my trust in thee. Let integrity and uprightness preserve me; for I wait on thee.

Hebrews 10:22-23
Let us draw near with a true heart in full assurance of faith, having our hearts sprinkled from an evil conscience, and our bodies washed with pure water. Let us hold fast the profession of *our* faith without wavering; (for he *is* faithful that promised;

Hebrews 9:14
How much more shall the blood of Christ, who through the

eternal Spirit offered himself without spot to God, purge your conscience from dead works to serve the living God?

2 Corinthians 10:4-5
For the weapons of our warfare *are* not carnal, but mighty through God to the pulling down of strong holds; Casting down imaginations, and every high thing that exalteth itself against the knowledge of God, and bringing into captivity every thought to the obedience of Christ;

Isaiah 54:4
Fear not; for thou shalt not be ashamed: neither be thou confounded; for thou shalt not be put to shame: for thou shalt forget the shame of thy youth,

Isaiah 43:18-19
Remember ye not the former things, neither consider the things of old. Behold, I will do a new thing; now it shall spring forth; shall ye not know it?

☙☙☙☙☙☙☙☙☙☙☙☙☙☙

Sickness
You say: Can I be healed? I have been sick a long time.
God says: I am the God who heals.

Jeremiah 33:6
Behold, I will bring it health and cure, and I will cure them, and will reveal unto them the abundance of peace and truth.

Matthew 4:23
And Jesus went about all Galilee, teaching in their synagogues, and preaching the gospel of the kingdom, and healing all manner of sickness and all manner of disease among the people.

Exodus 15:26
And said, If thou wilt diligently hearken to the voice of the LORD thy God, and wilt do that which is right in his sight, and wilt give ear to his commandments, and keep all his statutes, I will put none of these diseases upon thee, which I have brought upon the Egyptians: for I *am* the LORD that healeth thee.

Psalms 103:2-3
Bless the LORD, O my soul, and forget not all his benefits: Who forgiveth all thine iniquities; who healeth all thy diseases.

Isaiah 53:3-5
He is despised and rejected of men; a man of sorrows, and acquainted with grief: and we hid as it were *our* faces from him; he was despised, and we esteemed him not. Surely he hath borne our griefs, and carried our sorrows: yet we did esteem him stricken, smitten of God, and afflicted. But he *was* wounded for our transgressions, *he was* bruised for our iniquities: the chastisement of our peace *was* upon him; and with his stripes we are healed.

ଔଔଔଔଔଔଔଔଔଔଔଔଔଔଔ

Sorrow

<u>You say</u>: Will my heart ever feel happy again?
<u>God says</u>: There is joy for tomorrow. Trust me.

Isaiah 60:20
for the LORD shall be thine everlasting light, and the days of thy mourning shall be ended.

Jeremiah 31:12
Therefore they shall come and sing in the height of Zion, and shall flow together to the goodness of the LORD, for wheat, and for wine, and for oil, and for the young of the flock and of the

herd: and their soul shall be as a watered garden; and they shall not sorrow any more at all.

Isaiah 53:3-5
He is despised and rejected of men; a man of sorrows, and acquainted with grief: and we hid as it were *our* faces from him; he was despised, and we esteemed him not. Surely he hath borne our griefs, and carried our sorrows: yet we did esteem him stricken, smitten of God, and afflicted. But he *was* wounded for our transgressions, *he was* bruised for our iniquities: the chastisement of our peace *was* upon him; and with his stripes we are healed.

Isaiah 35:10
And the ransomed of the LORD shall return, and come to Zion with songs and everlasting joy upon their heads: they shall obtain joy and gladness, and sorrow and sighing shall flee away.

രുളുളുളുളുളുളുളുളുളുളുളുളു

Unloved
<u>**You say**</u>: "Nobody really loves me"
<u>**God says**</u>: I love you

John 3:16
For God so loved the world that he gave his one and only Son, that whoever believes in him shall not perish but have eternal life. NIV

<u>**You say**</u>: "It's not worth it, I'm not worth it."
<u>**God says**</u>: "It will be worth it and so are you."

Roman 8:28
And we know that all things work together for good to them that love God, to them who are the called according to his purpose.

You say: "I feel all alone."
God says: "I will never leave you or forsake you."

Genesis 2:18
And the LORD God said, It is not good that the man should be alone; I will make him an help meet for him.

Hebrews 13:5
Let your conversation be without covetousness; [and be] content with such things as ye have: for he hath said, I will never leave thee, nor forsake thee.

1 Peter 5:7
Casting all your care upon him; for he careth for you.

Psalms 34:18
The LORD [is] nigh unto them that are of a broken heart; and saveth such as be of a contrite spirit.

Proverbs 18:1
Through desire a man, having separated himself, seeketh [and] intermeddleth with all wisdom.

John 16:32-33
Behold, the hour cometh, yea, is now come, that ye shall be scattered, every man to his own, and shall leave me alone: and yet I am not alone, because the Father is with me.

Ecclesiastes 4:9-10
Two [are] better than one; because they have a good reward for their labour. For if they fall, the one will lift up his fellow...

Psalms 73:23
Nevertheless I [am] continually with thee: thou hast holden [me] by my right hand.

Psalms 23:4
Yea, though I walk through the valley of the shadow of death, I will fear no evil: for thou [art] with me; thy rod and thy staff they comfort me.

1 Corinthians 7:32-35
But I would have you without carefulness. He that is unmarried careth for the things that belong to the Lord, how he may please the Lord: (Read More...)

2 Corinthians 1:3-4
Blessed [be] God, even the Father of our Lord Jesus Christ, the Father of mercies, and the God of all comfort;   Hebrews 13:5 God has said, "Never will I leave you; never will I forsake you."

ઉ૪ઉ૪ઉ૪ઉ૪ઉ૪ઉ૪ઉ૪ઉ૪ઉ૪ઉ૪ઉ૪

Weariness
<u>**You say**</u>: "I'm too tired"
<u>**God says**</u>: "I will give you rest."

Matthew 11:28-30
Come to me, all you who are weary and burdened, and I will give you rest. Take my yoke upon you and learn from me, for I am gentle and humble in heart, and you will find rest for your souls. For my yoke is easy and my burden is light. NIV

<u>**You say**</u>: "I can't go on"
<u>**God says**</u>: "My grace is sufficient."

II Corinthians 12:9-10
But he said to me, "My grace is sufficient for you, for my power is made perfect in weakness." Therefore I will boast all the more gladly about my weaknesses, so that Christ's power may rest on

me. That is why, for Christ's sake, I delight in weaknesses, in insults, in hardships, in persecutions, in difficulties. For when I am weak, then I am strong. NIV

ଔଔଔଔଔଔଔଔଔଔଔଔଔଔଔଔ

Worry

<u>**You say**</u>: "There are so many things in my life that I worry about."
<u>**God says**</u>: "Cast all your cares on me."

Luke 6:47-48
Whosoever cometh to me, and heareth my sayings, and doeth them, I will shew you to whom he is like: He is like a man which built an house, and digged deep, and laid the foundation on a rock: and when the flood arose, the stream beat vehemently upon that house, and could not shake it: for it was founded upon a rock.

Matthew 6:25-34
Therefore I say unto you, Take no thought for your life, what ye shall eat, or what ye shall drink; nor yet for your body, what ye shall put on. Is not the life more than meat, and the body than raiment? Behold the fowls of the air: for they sow not, neither do they reap, nor gather into barns; yet your heavenly Father feedeth them. Are ye not much better than they? Which of you by taking thought can add one cubit unto his stature? And why take ye thought for raiment? Consider the lilies of the field, how they grow; they toil not, neither do they spin: And yet I say unto you, That even Solomon in all his glory was not arrayed like one of these. Wherefore, if God so clothe the grass of the field, which to day is, and to morrow is cast into the oven, *shall he* not much more *clothe* you, O ye of little faith? Therefore take no thought, saying, What shall we eat? or, What shall we drink? or, Wherewithal shall we be clothed? (For after all these things do

the Gentiles seek:) for your heavenly Father knoweth that ye have need of all these things. But seek ye first the kingdom of God, and his righteousness; and all these things shall be added unto you. Take therefore no thought for the morrow: for the morrow shall take thought for the things of itself. Sufficient unto the day *is* the evil thereof.

Philippines 4:6-7

Be careful for nothing; but in every thing by prayer and supplication with thanksgiving let your requests be made known unto God. And the peace of God, which passeth all understanding, shall keep your hearts and minds through Christ Jesus.

1 Peter 5:7

Casting all your care upon him; for he careth for you.

Isaiah 43:1-3

Fear not: for I have redeemed thee, I have called *thee* by thy name; thou *art* mine. When thou passest through the waters, I *will be* with thee; and through the rivers, they shall not overflow thee: when thou walkest through the fire, thou shalt not be burned; neither shall the flame kindle upon thee. For I *am* the LORD thy God, the Holy One of Israel, thy Saviour.

John 14:27

Peace I leave with you, my peace I give unto you: not as the world giveth, give I unto you. Let not your heart be troubled, neither let it be afraid.

You say: "I'm always worried and frustrated"
God says: "Cast all your cares on me."

I Peter 5:7

Cast all your anxiety on him because he cares for you. NIV

You Feel Stupid

You say: "I can't Study God's word. I don't understand. The Bible is too confusing."
God says : "I will give you wisdom as you read my word."

1 Corinthians 2:9-10
But as it is written, Eye hath not seen, nor ear heard, neither have entered into the heart of man, the things which God hath prepared for them that love him. But God hath revealed *them* unto us by his Spirit: for the Spirit searcheth all things, yea, the deep things of God.

1 Corinthians 2:16
For who hath known the mind of the Lord, that he may instruct him? But we have the mind of Christ.

Romans 12:2
And be not conformed to this world: but be ye transformed by the renewing of your mind, that ye may prove what *is* that good, and acceptable, and perfect, will of God.

John 14:26
But the Comforter, *which is* the Holy Ghost, whom the Father will send in my name, he shall teach you all things, and bring all things to your remembrance, whatsoever I have said unto you.

Psalms 27:11
Teach me thy way, O LORD, and lead me in a plain path,
You say: "I can't figure things out"
God says: "I will direct your steps."

Proverbs 3:5-6
Trust in the LORD with all your heart and lean not on your own

understanding; in all your ways acknowledge him, and he will make your paths straight. NIV

You say: "I'm not smart enough"
God says: "I give you wisdom."

I Corinthians 1:30
It is because of him that you are in Christ Jesus, who has become for us wisdom from God-- that is, our righteousness, holiness and redemption. NIV

You say: "I can't do it"
God says: "You can do all things with my strength."

Philippians 4:13
I can do all things through Christ which strengtheneth me.

You say: "I'm not able"
God says: "I am able."

II Corinthians 9:8
And God is able to make all grace abound toward you; that ye, always having all sufficiency in all things, may abound to every good work.
You say: "I can't manage"
God says: "I will supply all your needs."

Philippians 4:19
But my God shall supply all your need according to his riches in glory by Christ Jesus.

ACKNOLDGEMENTS

I want to thank my friends Christine, Melissa, Judith, and my sister, Cheri for all of their help and input. My husband, Fred spent hours helping me with formatting. I am grateful for all of their help.

Most of all I am thankful for the Holy Spirit's help and His inspiration. Every day that I would write a chapter, the Lord would give me new ideas. I never would have written this had it not been for Him.

OTHER BOOKS BY DEBBY DAVIS

Suddenly
Keepers of Salt
Keepers of Salt Study Guide
The Only Way Out Is In
Peace
Poems To Live By Dog of Blue
Poems To Live By Any Ol Bush
Storm Walker
Because God Said So

IF YOU WOULD LIKE TO HAVE DEBBY SPEAK TO YOUR CHURCH OR GATHERING CONTACT HER AT DEBBY@DAVISMISSION.COM

CREATURES OF THE FOREST

37444012R00091

Made in the USA
Middletown, DE
28 February 2019